MR. BLACK LABOR

MR. BLACK LABOR

The Story of A. Philip Randolph,
Father of the Civil Rights Movement

by DANIEL S. DAVIS

INTRODUCTION BY BAYARD RUSTIN

E. P. DUTTON & CO., INC.   NEW YORK

Published simultaneously in Canada by Clarke,
Irwin & Company Limited, Toronto and Vancouver

SBN: 0-525-35325-9   LCC: 72-182599

Designed by Hilda Scott
Printed in the U.S.A.
First Edition

For Yona

Contents

	Introduction by *Bayard Rustin*	ix
1	Growing Up in Dixie	1
2	"The Most Dangerous Negro in America"	11
3	The Labor Movement	26
4	Struggle for a Black Union	41
5	The Battle with Pullman	52
6	Black Labor Power	66
7	Fighting from Within	80
8	The National Negro Congress	91
9	The March on Washington Movement	100
10	War on Two Fronts	113
11	End of the Jim Crow Army	123
12	"Keep Up the Pressure"	133
13	Marching for Jobs and Freedom	145
14	Father of the Civil Rights Movement	156
	Selected Bibliography	165
	Index	169

Photos appear between pages 112 and 113.

Introduction by Bayard Rustin

A. PHILIP RANDOLPH, more so than any other man, has earned the right to be called the Father of the Civil Rights Movement. He led protests at a time, early in this century, when protests were neither fashionable nor safe. He conceived and popularized the strategies which brought black Americans their most profound and far-reaching legislative achievements. And his philosophy of personal conduct and action served, not only to define his own life, but to shape and provide substance for the entire movement for racial freedom, social justice, and economic equality.

But for those whose lives and spirits have been committed to these struggles, Mr. Randolph has meant much more. For myself and many others, he has been the spiritual father of civil rights and social activism; a man who translated our energies into positive action and tempered our enthusiasm with a sense of responsibility to the movement. I have been fortunate in enjoying a long and close personal relationship with Mr. Randolph dating from the

time when, coming from home in Pennsylvania, I moved
to New York eager to participate in the civil rights movement but lacking direction and a coherent set of principles. It was Mr. Randolph who impressed upon me the
importance of those principles around which any successful social movement must be based: adherence to democracy, non-violence, and integration.

Perhaps Mr. Randolph's greatest strength was his
ability to stand alone, without allies, lacking in money or
the hope of funds with which to operate an organization,
nurtured only by convictions and vision. The loneliness of
those early days of struggle are difficult for us to conceive
of today. The very concept of racial integration, now an
ingrained part of our legal code and increasingly accepted
in custom and practice, was alien to a substantial majority
of Americans, both north and south.

Mr. Randolph became familiar with disappointment
and defeat in those early years. No one would have blamed
him for abandoning a fight which seemed so hopeless.
Nor would he have been blamed for feeling hatred for
whites and all the institutions they influence and control.
He had occasion to fight them all—corporations who
treated their workers with all the magnanimity of feudal
land barons; a military leadership unrelenting in its opposition to racial integration; government figures, from
Presidents on down, who found the Negro's cause the
most painless and available sacrifice to political expedi-
ency.

And never was a man more isolated than in Mr. Randolph's lifelong campaign to bring black workers into the
American trade union movement. He provoked the opposition of the most powerful captains of industry, who
feared the loss of what had been a plentiful supply of

cheap, exploitable labor. He was opposed by many of the unions themselves. And he had to confront a strongly implanted current of anti-labor sentiment within the black community.

Yet Mr. Randolph never succumbed to despair and held firm to his convictions despite the frustrations and bitter defeats. There are now 2.5 million black workers in the trade union movement, earning on an average 50 percent more than their unorganized brothers. Blacks are taking an increasingly large percentage of union leadership roles. The barriers of discrimination are falling even in those unions where bias was the most deeply embedded and blatant. For its part, the labor movement has become the most effective and reliable ally of the civil rights movement and has been the driving force behind most crucial civil rights legislation.

The close relationship between the civil rights and labor movements might have never come about had Mr. Randolph taken the easy road of separatism. However, he always realized that separatism, whether espoused by Marcus Garvey or latter-day nationalists, is grounded in fantasy and myth despite its emotional appeal to an oppressed people.

He chose instead the tortuous task of leading blacks into the mainstream of American society. His understanding of weakness and prejudice, and his ability to forgive these human failings, so often displayed on a personal level to friends, carried over to his relationship with whites. Despite virulent criticism and unyielding opposition, he never lost sight of the realistic: black people, he realized, could never advance without the good feelings and assistance of many whites.

It was through Mr. Randolph's leadership that black

Americans first demonstrated that they could deal as equals with the most powerful and influential corporate institutions. And in doing so, Mr. Randolph's organization, the Brotherhood of Sleeping Car Porters, overcame a tradition of discrimination in addition to the obstacles which confront every labor organization.

And he proved, on numerous occasions, that black people could organize and struggle, militantly but nonviolently, against oppression. While the 1963 March on Washington remains fresh in the memories of all Americans, few recall that the first March on Washington movement in 1941 resulted in a presidential order ending discrimination in defense industries and a later campaign led by Mr. Randolph was responsible for President Truman's banning discrimination in the armed services.

We are still very much in need of the wisdom, vision, and leadership of A. Philip Randolph. Perhaps now, when the problems facing blacks are much more complex, are we in need of those qualities which enabled him to stand above others: his judgment, his compassion, his refusal to compromise basic convictions because they are temporarily unfashionable, and his fearlessness. These are uncommon qualities in a man. But today, living in a nation and world in turmoil, we need men like A. Philip Randolph more than ever if we are to build a society based on justice and live at peace with ourselves.

May 31, 1972
New York, New York

MR. BLACK LABOR

CHAPTER ONE

Growing Up in Dixie

"Is your dad at home, Asa?" the tall, tense black man said to the boy playing marbles in front of a small frame house in Jacksonville, Florida.

Asa Philip Randolph and his older brother James barely looked up from their game. "He's inside, with Mom," they answered, and the serious-faced man trudged up the worn steps. Soon he was followed by other men, coming in groups of twos and threes, speaking to each other in hushed tones.

The boys grew curious, and went into the house to find out what was happening. Their father, Reverend James Randolph, sat in the sparsely furnished living room talking with the men. Fragments of conversation reached them in the hallway: "guns" and "mob" and "jailhouse," and then the word that struck terror into their young hearts—"lynching."

Later that night James Randolph went into his bedroom and came back with two guns. He put one of them into the hands of his wife, kissed her on the cheek, and then disappeared into the humid blackness of the night.

As their mother tucked the boys into bed, she explained what had happened. A black man had been arrested, charged with a crime. Some white men in town were angry and wanted to take the law into their own hands. It was something that was going on all over the South—mobs of white people would refuse to let a black man get a fair trial. They would pull him from his jail cell, torture him, and then hang him from a tree. It was called "lynching," and it was one of the many ways southern whites kept black people in fear. Any bold black man who tried to do something that challenged white supremacy was labeled "uppity," and knew that he too might soon fall victim to a lynch mob's vengeance.

"Your father," she explained, "isn't going to let that happen here. That man is going to get a fair trial. If he's guilty, he'll go to prison, but your father and his friends are determined that there will be no lynching in this town."

Asa lay awake that night, remembering his mother's words. Reverend Randolph would take his boys to hear him preach in the country churches on Sundays, and Asa remembered that he often told his congregations that black people had to stick together and protect each other. "These days are hard ones for black folk," their father would say, "and unless we stand up for our rights, they'll be a lot worse."

Militancy was a family tradition. Their mother's father was a lumber dealer, so light in skin color that people who did not know often mistook him for a white man. But he was proud of being a Negro, and never was tempted to "pass" to escape discrimination. White people always treated him with respect, and called him Mr. Robinson, instead of "boy" or "Robby." Perhaps it was because of his proud, dignified manner of dress and speech that they treated him so differently. Or perhaps it was the gun he always carried in his belt. He never used it, but it was a warning to racists not to try any of their white-supremacy tricks on him.

Now, that hot summer's night in 1898, the old man's daughter was sitting up all night with a shotgun at her side to defend her home, and his son-in-law was one of several black defenders of law ringing the jailhouse to keep a fellow black man from being lynched.

Darkest night slowly crept away, and the feeble first rays of the morning sun filtered through the boys' bedroom window. The sharp sound of boots crackling against the gravel path in front of the house sent both boys scurrying to the window. It was their father. They burst from their room, pajama tops flapping behind them. They flew into their father's arms as he walked in the door. He hugged them gently, a smile on his weary face.

"Well," he said in a voice raw with sleeplessness, "we won. About a dozen of us just stood in a line around the jailhouse, with our guns ready. Some of the white folks came up to me and told me that it was a good thing—our standing up to make sure there would be no lynching. Other white folks looked at us funny like, and then walked away shaking their heads. They might have been planning a lynching bee, but when they saw us ready for business, why they just changed their minds."

Then he leaned forward and said in more serious tones: "Boys, this shows what can happen when black folk stick together. Together we're strong, separately we're weak. Don't you ever forget what happened here last night."

And Asa never did forget that night.

Asa Philip Randolph was born on April 15, 1889—just twenty-four short years after the end of the Civil War— in Crescent City, Florida, a small town outside Jacksonville. He was called Asa as a child but later preferred Phil. Two years after, the Randolphs moved to Jacksonville, where Philip grew up under the keen guidance of his strong father, his proud mother, and his brilliant brother James.

Reverend Randolph was a minister without a permanent church. Many black communities in the South were too poor to afford a church and a preacher. So black ministers would work at odd jobs during the week and then on Sundays hold services at humble rural churches or in city storefront churches.

Reverend Randolph was one of these ministers. He was a preacher in the African Methodist Episcopal Church, one of the largest nationwide churches. It was founded shortly after the American Revolution by black people who refused to attend segregated white churches. Some blacks continued to go to the white churches, sitting in fenced-off sections in the back. But most wanted nothing to do with a church that spoke hypocritically of Christian equality while discriminating against black worshipers. Sunday mornings found them in all-black churches listening to black preachers and singing the hymns and songs of an oppressed people whose God would cleanse their wounds and salve their souls.

Very often, Reverend Randolph would not be paid in

cash for his preaching. Instead, the congregations of poor farmers would give him chickens, vegetables, or sometimes, just a humble thank you.

During the week, he worked at home as a tailor and clothes cleaner. Mrs. Randolph helped; she sewed and waited on customers. Reverend Randolph did the pressing, tailoring, and delivered the finished clothing to his customers.

Phil was growing up at a time when black people's sufferings were increasing daily. When his father was a boy, blacks had just been freed from slavery. In the period known as Reconstruction, they were given the right to vote and began attending schools for the first time. Black people could walk the streets without fear, and could enter any hotel or restaurant, or ride any streetcar or riverboat, on an equal basis with whites.

Most black people were very poor, and many continued to work on the same plantations they toiled in slavery. But there was a surface equality that gave the promise of becoming, in time, full equality with white people. The Reconstruction experiment, however, only lasted for ten years. By 1876 the northern reformers who led the fight for black freedom tired of the struggle and turned their backs on the Negro. The southern states that had black people sitting in their legislatures and in high offices were now firmly in the hands of conservatives, many of whom won their elections by threats and through armed terror. They couldn't restore slavery, but they were determined to keep the black man out of politics and confined to the bottom of the ladder.

By the time Philip was born, their counter-revolution was in full swing. The hooded Ku Klux Klan terrorized and lynched blacks who stepped out of line, while state after state began passing laws restricting the rights of black people. All the while, the North looked the other way, refusing to help the blacks the war had set free, even though the Constitution said black people had the same rights as whites.

In 1896 the Supreme Court ruled that it was legal to have separate school systems for white and black children, and that was the signal for the whole South to set up rigid segregation through what were known as Jim Crow laws separating the races.

So Philip and his brother went to an all-black school and when Philip, who inherited his father's love of books, tried to enter the public library, he was turned away. Only white people could use the library, he was told, and he had to leave without the books he so dearly wanted to read.

The Randolph family refused to be Jim Crowed. There was little they could do to stop it, of course, but they resisted segregation as best they could. When Jacksonville's streetcars were segregated, the family decided they'd never ride them again. Reverend Randolph spoke up on Sunday mornings in church, telling his parishioners that riding in the "colored" section was degrading. "We pay the same fare as white folks do," he said, "so we too should be able to sit wherever we want. By not riding the streetcar you can keep your dignity and punish the company for segregating us."

The world outside the Randolph house was harsh and brutal. But inside, though they were poor, love and warmth ruled. Although they never had a formal education, both of the boys' parents could read. That was unusual for poor blacks brought up on farms in those days, but then, the Randolphs were an unusual family.

Neither poverty nor segregation could break the strong family bonds.

The Randolph boys learned to read long before they started school. Their father would sit with them each evening, teaching them the alphabet, then words and sentences, and finally, the Bible. Young Philip read each chapter of the Bible over and over again under his father's watchful eye.

"What do you think that means, Phil?" his father would ask. And Phil would discuss the text until his father was convinced he knew and understood it. Then they'd turn to the next chapter and repeat the process.

He learned to love the worn pages of his father's books, and he would spend hours reading the Bible, Shakespeare, and other classics. It was the language that held him spellbound. The rich, rolling words drew him into another world, a world of great thoughts and lofty ideals. Each day he would come home from school, gobble down his glass of milk, race out to play with the neighborhood kids, and then come home to sit with his father's books, reading until his mother would chase him off to bed.

The books supplied him with many heroes, but his favorite was Paul, one of Jesus's first followers and a founder of Christianity. Phil had his doubts about religion, but the story of this man who accepted the teachings of Jesus at a time when most people considered them subversive, gripped him. Paul endured many hardships; people scorned him and he was thrown into jail. But still he believed, and spread the Gospel to all who would listen.

Philip identified with Paul. He knew that segregation was evil, and felt he had to do something to end it. He realized that, like Paul, he would be threatened, despised, and perhaps imprisoned. But the story of a man who, nearly two thousand years ago, stuck to his beliefs and tried to convince others of their truth, gripped young Philip's imagination.

The family was too poor to be able to afford the luxury of two young scholars sitting around the house devouring their father's books. So James and Phil did odd jobs around the neighborhood, turning their wages over to their father at the end of the week. The boys were very close and did everything together. James was a whiz in school—the smartest boy in his class. But Philip was also pretty smart, and as they went into town to their jobs, they would play quiz games about black history to make the long walk seem shorter.

"Who was the first black man to die in the American Revolution?" Phil would ask.

"Crispus Attucks," James would shoot back. "That was easy. Now you name three black slaves who led big revolts."

And Phil would knot his brows in thought. "Nat Turner, Denmark Vesey, and . . . uh . . . and. . . ." "Gabriel Prosser," James would say triumphantly. "How could you forget him?" And the boys would laugh and start another round of "guess who."

Their first jobs were as newsboys in downtown Jacksonville. They would go to the newspaper office to pick up their supply of papers, sometimes having to fight off other boys who tried to keep them back. But James and Philip were pretty handy with their fists, especially when they knew that if they didn't get to the front of the line they'd have no papers to sell, and that might mean nothing on the dinner table that night.

Philip later delivered packages for a grocery store, and his good manners and speed made him a favorite of the customers. As he grew older and stronger, he did heavier work, shoveling dirt at construction sites, and laying railroad tracks.

Most black youngsters in those days never went past elementary school, but Reverend Randolph was determined that his children would get the best education possible. He had dreams of Philip becoming a great preacher. Already the young man was showing a gift for speaking. He would practice reading the Bible aloud, and spent many hours reciting parts from the plays of Shakespeare. His voice was deep and strong, perfect for the pulpit. Phil even began organizing shows featuring himself in dramatic readings with friends who sang, danced, and told stories. These were very popular, further evidence to Reverend Randolph that his younger son had a dramatic gift that could draw people to the church.

So Philip attended Cookman Institute in Jacksonville, studying Latin, mathematics, and other subjects normally taught only to white youngsters. He became interested in current events, and would often expound on the evils of segregation to his classmates. The more he studied, the more there grew within him the desire to help his people achieve full equality.

His broad reading equipped him to look critically at the twisted society of the South. Despite his father's wishes, he knew he wouldn't be a preacher. His doubts about religion were becoming too strong.

One of his favorite authors was a brilliant black sociologist, W. E. B. Du Bois. Du Bois rejected the dominant black thinking of the period that said blacks should accept the evils of the white South and overcome its prejudices by demonstrating humbleness.

Du Bois was saying something radically different, and his message lit sparks in Philip's searching mind. Du Bois called for more militant black leadership, and stressed education as the key to the future. "The Negro race, like all races, is going to be saved by its exceptional men," he wrote. "The talented tenth of the Negro race must be made leaders of thought . . . among their people."

Here was Philip's mission—to be one of that talented tenth that would pioneer through the forests of discrimination; one of that small band of educated black people who would lift the masses of blacks to a state of equality.

Years before that, when still a young boy, Philip would play games of fighting for Negro rights. "You keep that up and you'll be lynched," a friend told him, only half-joking.

"Oh no I won't," Philip answered. "I'll go north and fight.'

Philip remembered the prophetic incident as he clutched his small suitcase and stared at the passing South from the windows of the northbound railroad car. He was on his way to New York and a new life.

CHAPTER TWO

"The Most Dangerous Negro in America"

PHILIP arrived in New York in 1906, a tall, rawboned country boy filled with the excitement of the sights and sounds of the big city. It was, in his eyes, the capital of the world. Nowhere else could there be so many people, such tall buildings, or so many motorcars that charged down the broad avenues at twice the speed of the horse-drawn carts still common on the streets of Jacksonville.

He was not a complete stranger to the city. The summer before, he had worked on a steamship that chugged its way up the Atlantic coast, docking in New York. There, he lived with a cousin while working at odd jobs before returning home to finish school.

School. That was what he was here for. As soon as he was settled, Philip enrolled in night courses at the College of the City of New York. He studied economics, philosophy, and sociology, and the more he read and studied, the more convinced he became that the country was sick and it would take more than his father's religious beliefs to cure it.

He was a good student, reading everything he could lay his hands on. In class, although tired from a long day's work, he questioned his teachers closely, seeking to squeeze every drop of knowledge they possessed. Often, the bell ending the class was just Phil's signal to rush to his professor's desk to pump him with questions and arguments. One of his teachers was the famous philosopher, Morris Raphael Cohen, who enjoyed the bright, aggressive young man from the South. Cohen helped Phil to sharpen his ideas and to think problems through, never simply accepting what the books said.

Many nights, Phil would spend long hours after class talking with his fellow students. They would discuss the ideas they were studying, and also the terrible conditions of poor people. Reformist ideas were in the air and Phil and his classmates were becoming convinced that the answer to America's problems was Socialism.

The Socialists seemed to be the only ones who cared about black people and working people. Phil believed that the big-business interests who controlled the country kept blacks and whites divided to dominate both groups. Racial hatreds, he said, were the result of modern capitalism. If blacks and whites would get together in unions and fight for higher wages for everybody, they could break the power of the big trusts and monopolies. Then, a Socialist America would make sure that no one was exploited and that all were treated fairly.

This was the Socialists' view of the racial situation. Even in the South, Socialists declared that "the question of race superiority" was just a method of the "capitalist class to keep the workers divided." While both the Democratic and Republican parties were run by business interests and were openly opposed to civil rights, including the right of blacks to vote in the South, the Socialists were openly welcoming blacks as members.

Their founding convention, in 1901, called on black workers to join in "the world movement for emancipation." Yes, thought Philip, black people weren't really emancipated in 1863, they just became wage slaves in a system that continued to oppress them. Only when white and black workers get together to change the system that exploits us both will we be really free.

But while dreaming of a new and better future, Phil had to work to pay the rent and to buy food. His first job didn't last long. He was hired to write pamphlets for an employment office that found work for black maids fresh from the South. When he found that his boss was cheating the inexperienced young girls who weren't familiar with city life, he quit.

For five years he worked as a porter in the offices of the Consolidated Edison Company. Few of the executives there noticed the silent black man pushing a broom down the silent hallways, a book sticking out of his back pocket. None of them suspected that someday that young man would sit with Presidents and lead hundreds of thousands of people. Now he was just a menial employee who would sometimes sneak off into a washroom to read books whose ideas would someday change the country.

Phil had other jobs as well, but his fierce devotion to the principles of unionism got him fired time and again. For a while he worked as a waiter on a riverboat. The living quarters assigned to the men were dark, dirty, and cramped. They gave it the nickname, the "glory hole." When Phil organized the other workers on the boat to protest their terrible conditions, he was labeled a "troublemaker" and fired.

He worked as a waiter in a Jersey City railroad restaurant and as an elevator operator. The story was the same. He would try to organize the workers, the bosses would get wind of it, erupt in anger, and send him packing. Only hard, low-paying jobs were open to black men and, for all his learning, Phil could not find a decent job. But he didn't care. He had a mission in life: to better the lot of the black people and poor people he worked with.

One of his best friends shared his views. He was Chandler Owen, a short, round man whose penetrating eyes and sharp tongue stamped him for leadership. Owen was a graduate student at Columbia University and, like Phil, a Socialist who believed the path of salvation for black people lay in organized unionism.

Together the two young men formed an employment bureau which they called "The Brotherhood" to symbolize their belief in the brotherhood of working people. Most of the people who came to their small office were new arrivals from the South. They knew farming, but didn't know much about city ways or how to do the jobs that were available in the city. So Phil and Chandler did more than simply send them to an employer. They trained them in work habits and taught the job-seekers how to get along in an atmosphere so vastly different from the one they had left.

They also tried to organize workers into unions. Phil, who had worked as an elevator operator, was anxious to get all the black elevator operators in the city together in a union that would demand a living wage and shorter hours. He and Chandler went from building to building talking with elevator men, and signed them up for the union. Within three weeks, they had six hundred members who demanded an 8-hour day and $18 per week. But new members were slow to join, a strike was threatened but never took place, and the drive for an elevator union collapsed.

Their organizing efforts brought them to the attention of the Headwaiters and Sidewaiters Society of Greater New York, a union of black waiters. Randolph and Owen were asked to publish a magazine for the union, and they eagerly agreed. Both men wrote well, and were anxious to start a periodical that would spread their ideas among working people. They called it *The Hotel Messenger*.

But as they became more familiar with the working conditions in hotel dining rooms, they were shocked to find that headwaiters, who were in charge of the serving staff, were cheating the workers they supervised. They discovered that headwaiters bought uniforms from a wholesaler and then forced other employees to buy them at two and even three times their price. In effect, it was a tax or bribe for the lesser waiters to keep their jobs.

The two men were furious. Here was exploitation of poor working men and women. And it wasn't done by rich capitalists. It was done by other black working people who even had their own union! Randolph and Owen decided to expose this corruption, and one day in the fall of 1917, the union's members opened *The Hotel Messenger* to find the whole sordid story splashed across its pages. The sidewaiters, who were the victims of the practice of dealing in uniforms, chuckled with delight that the story had finally come out, but the headwaiters, who really ran the union, were furious. As they knew they would be, Randolph and Owen were fired, but they had witnessed the power of the press and, when they left, they took the magazine with them.

Dropping the word "Hotel" from the title, and with

credit from a Brooklyn printer, the young men launched *The Messenger,* destined to become one of the important radical periodicals of the day. It started life in two tiny rooms on the third floor of an old Harlem brownstone. Here Randolph and Owen would sit at their secondhand desks beating out their visions of a Socialist future on an old battered typewriter. From time to time they'd pause in thought, looking at the paint peeling from the ceilings and at the dusty floor covered with disorganized stacks of files and clippings.

The Messenger came out each month, and just below its title was the slogan, "The Only Radical Negro Magazine in America." The tone of the magazine was angry, and there was much to be angry about in the America of 1917. Black people were robbed of their rights, had few job opportunities, and the country had just entered a bloody European war many people thought was none of its business. The government in Washington was headed by Virginia-born Woodrow Wilson, who introduced segregation into federal offices. Black officials and employees of the government were dismissed from their jobs, were forced to drink from separate water fountains and to use separate eating and toilet facilities in government buildings. Meanwhile, lynching in the South continued unchecked, and the vicious Ku Klux Klan was beginning to spread its message of hate all across the country. Black Southerners were flocking northward to find jobs in war industries, and found themselves forced to live in run-down ghettos. This migration from the farms of the South to the big cities of the North led to agitation that erupted in several race riots.

Indeed, there was plenty to be angry about, and the

militant young Socialists who edited *The Messenger* were outspoken in their denunciations of American life, racism, and even the old-line black leaders. Their chief target was the capitalist system of private enterprise for private profit.

Randolph wrote in *The Messenger:*

Capitalism is a system under which a small class of private individuals makes profits out of the labor of the masses by virtue of their ownership of the machinery and sources of production and exchange. . . . It is to the interests of the employer to work the laborer long hours and to pay as low wages as possible. . . . Hence, the conflict between capitalists and the workers. . . . Socialism would deprive individuals of the power to make fortunes out of the labor of other individuals by virtue of their ownership of the machinery which the worker must use in order to live.

He saw racism as a part of the capitalist system and thundered in *The Messenger*:

If the employers can keep the white and black dogs, on account of race prejudice, fighting over a bone, the yellow capitalist dog will get away with the bone—the bone of profits.

Revolution must come. By that we mean a complete change in the organization of society. Just as absence of industrial democracy is productive of riots and race clashes, so the introduction of industrial democracy will be the longest step toward removing the cause. When no profits are to be made from race friction, no one will any longer be interested in stirring up race prejudice. The quickest way to stop a thing or to destroy an institution is to destroy the profitableness of that institution. The capitalist system must go and its going must be hastened by the workers themselves.

The Phil Randolph of 1917 sounded very much like the radical black militants of the 1960's and 1970's. He wrote, in words that could come from a Black Panther manifesto:

The solution will not follow the meeting of white and Negro leaders in love feasts, who pretend, like the African ostrich, that nothing is wrong, because their heads are buried in the sand.

On the economic field, industry must be socialized, and land must be nationalized, which will thereby remove the motive for creating strife between the races. . . .

The people must organize, own and control their press.

The church must be converted into an educational forum.

The stage and screen must be controlled by the people.

The Messenger was very rough on the established black leadership of the country. Of course, they rejected the moderates, led by friends and associates of Booker T. Washington, who had died only two years before, in 1915. But they were just as vicious in their denunciation of W. E. B. Du Bois and his National Association for the Advancement of Colored People, which was founded in 1910 by white and black Socialist reformers.

Randolph had become disillusioned with Du Bois because, after the founding of the NAACP, Du Bois' organizational responsibilities forced him to a more moderate stance. Du Bois' Socialism was of the reformist variety, much closer to that of the intellectual elite with whom he associated than Randolph's trade-union-oriented beliefs. By the time Randolph started *The Messenger,* they differed strongly on the question of unionization, and later, on the war.

One *Messenger* article, this time by Owen, denounced Du Bois for encouraging blacks to take any jobs they could get, even as strikebreakers. Many black workers at this time were faced by a terrible dilemma. White workers wouldn't allow them to join their unions, and when they went out on strike, employers would attempt to keep the factories open by using non-union black workers. Such strikebreakers were known as "scabs." Owen accused black leaders of "preaching the gospel of hate against labor unionism, when they should be explaining to the Negroes the necessity of allying themselves with the worker's motive power and weapon—the Labor Union and the Strike."

The unionism Randolph and Owen had in mind was not the unionism of the nation's dominant labor organization, the American Federation of Labor. They supported, instead, a radical union called the Industrial Workers of the World, which sought to join all workers into "One Big Union" that would change society. "The editors of *The Messenger*," Randolph wrote, "are not interested in Negroes getting more work. Negroes have too much work already. What we want Negroes to get is less work and more wages, with more leisure for study and recreation."

This kind of language was bound to lead to trouble, especially when the dynamic journalists mounted a full-scale attack on the war, which they labeled "the Imperialist Struggle." Randolph declared that the war had started because of the rivalry between France and England on one side, and Germany on the other, over the rich resources and markets of African and Asian colonies. He said he was a pacifist and morally opposed to national wars, and refused to serve in the army.

He fought the war in the pages of *The Messenger,* on Harlem street corners, and in speeches all over the country. America's role in the war, he said, was the height of hypocrisy. The official slogan spread by the government was that this was a war "to make the world safe for democracy." But Randolph and his band of radicals had only scorn for this. "What kind of democracy?" they asked. And since American democracy meant Jim Crow, lynching, and racism, the hollowness of the country's entry onto the world stage was apparent to many black citizens.

This was especially so when reports of discrimination and mistreatment of black soldiers filtered home. Blacks were segregated into all-Negro army units, often headed by white commanders from the South who despised the men and thought little of their capabilities. The American army, alarmed at the lack of racial prejudice among the French allies, forced French officials to prevent the black soldiers from being treated as equals.

Most of the segregated units were labor battalions of stevedores, road-builders, and similar maintenance crews. When blacks were given a chance to fight in the front lines, they did so well that the French high command formally requested that black units be assigned to fight alongside them, but such successes were treated with scorn by some Americans. One newspaper in Milwaukee wrote of the heroic blacks who spearheaded a major Allied victory: "Those two American colored regiments fought well, and it calls for special recognition. Is there no way of getting a cargo of watermelons over there?"

But racist stereotypes were only part of the problem. Friction between black soldiers and white communities in the South burst into bloody battles on more than one occasion. In 1917 black troopers and white civilians fought it out in a bloody riot in Houston that resulted in a mass murder trial. Thirteen of the soldiers were hanged and another forty-one sentenced to life imprisonment. Wartime tensions also led to race riots like that in East St. Louis, where 125 blacks were killed and hundreds injured at the hands of white mobs inflamed by labor troubles in the town.

After that horrible incident, fifteen thousand black New Yorkers marched down Fifth Avenue in a silent protest march, bearing signs that echoed Phil Randolph's position: "Mr. President, why not make America safe for Democracy?"

When he wasn't out on lecture tours or banging out fierce editorials for *The Messenger,* Randolph could be found on the corner of 135th Street and Lenox Avenue giving weekend soapbox speeches against the war and the capitalist system that led to it. His deep, sonorous voice rose above the din of the traffic as he carefully explained to the attentive groups of Harlemites just how the war was claiming poor people and black people as its victims.

He spoke at an anti-war rally in Cleveland in 1918. By this time he was a marked man, and government agents were following him as they did other "dangerous radicals." As Randolph launched into his usual attack on the war as a racist, hypocritical venture into imperialism and urged resistance to the draft laws, Justice Department agents mounted the platform and hauled him off to jail. He spent a few days in prison on a charge of obstructing the draft, but the case never came to trial and he was released. Despite the sure knowledge that further resistance to the war effort might land him in jail—this time for a longer period—he kept plugging away against the war in speeches and articles.

The end of the war brought renewed bitterness for black people. Instead of the nation honoring their loyalty through social and economic reforms, as some black leaders had hoped, the war's end was just the signal for new oppression. The summer of 1919 became known as the "Red Summer" because of the riots and lynchings that claimed blacks as victims. That year, seventy-six blacks were lynched, including some in army uniforms. A race riot in Chicago, which started when a black youth swam into the "white area" of a public beach and was stoned to death, claimed the lives of twenty-two blacks, sixteen whites, and left five hundred people injured.

Race riots spread like wildfire all across the country. Washington, D.C., itself was in the hands of white rioters who tore blacks from streetcars and offices and beat them. In many of these riots, including the one in the nation's capital, police openly sided with the rioters, and it took armed troops to bring the situation under control. Not until the mid-1960's was there another such outbreak of racially based rioting. The riots of the sixties were by predominately black crowds directing their anger against stores and property in ghetto neighborhoods; the 1919 outbreaks were started by white mobs out to kill and beat black people.

In many of the 1919 riots, blacks fought back, exhibiting a new spirit of resistance. *The Messenger* was all for this new spirit of what it called the "New Negro," the man who would stand up and fight for his rights. *Messenger* editorials, already harshly militant, took on a new stridency. In the July issue, the magazine featured a drawing that showed a burning victim of a lynch mob, with the flames forming a picture of the American flag. The U.S. Post Office moved swiftly and refused to let that issue of *The Messenger* be mailed. Another cartoon, showing armed blacks fighting in the European war as well as in the Washington riots, brought howls of protest from southern congressmen, who called on the government to seize the magazine and jail its editors.

Pressures of the war and rampant racism were pushing Randolph to militant revolutionary stands. In a "Thanksgiving Prayer" in the December *Messenger*, Randolph gave thanks for the Russian revolution and for the strikes and Communist revolutions that were taking place in many places in Europe and Asia, praying for "the new day dawning when we can celebrate a real thanksgiving in a world of labor, with peace and plenty for all."

Later, he was to change his mind about the Russian revolution, but in 1919 he still thought it would lead to Socialist equality for all in a new era of justice. Within a year or two it became apparent that the Bolshevik revolution would turn into a despotic dictatorship, and Randolph sided with the Democratic Socialists who rejected Communism.

Randolph and Owen, as uncompromising radicals, were easy targets for those who wanted to end all dissent. In 1919, when the Red Scare was launched, many people who had no thoughts of violent revolution, but who desired a more democratic America, found themselves victims of government suppression. The precious constitutional rights of freedom of speech and freedom of the press were brutally trampled as some publications were closed down and radicals were arrested simply for object-

ing to the injustices of the system. It was much like the
McCarthy era in the 1950's, as the witch-hunters went on
their search for "Reds" and trampled on constitutional
rights in the process.

But Randolph and Owen weren't about to be scared
into silence. Accused of being Bolsheviks (the popular
term for Communists), they replied in the pages of *The
Messenger:*

"If approval of the right to vote, based on service
instead of race and color, is Bolshevism, count us as
Bolshevists. If our approval of the abolition of pogroms
by the Bolsheviki is Bolshevism, stamp us again with that
epithet. If the demand for political and social equality is
Bolshevism, label us once more. . . ."

To the government agents, belief in political and social
equality for black people *was* proof of Bolshevism. Attorney General A. Mitchell Palmer declared that "A certain
class of Negro leaders . . . constitute themselves a determined and persistent source of radical opposition to
the Government and to the established rule of law and
order." He reached this conclusion because of their stand
in favor of radical revolutions in Europe, an "ill-
governed reaction toward race rioting" (which meant
they approved of blacks fighting back in self-defense),
their opposition to lynching, and "the more openly expressed demand for social equality."

Randolph and Owen were cited by the Attorney General as being among the dangerous black leaders, and he
claimed they were all the more dangerous because they
wrote in "fine, pure English, with a background of
scholarship," and were pushing for black equality.

Palmer's Red-hunters raided *The Messenger*'s offices
looking for subversive material which they could use to

jail the editors, but left only a bit dusty for their troubles. Federal agents hounded the two men, but no action was ever taken against them. Then, just as quickly as it had begun, the Red-hunting madness subsided and the agents were called off.

To be branded dangerous by such fanatical opponents to equal rights for black people was a high compliment, and Randolph had to be somewhat pleased by his status as a foe of the established order. When a special committee of the New York legislature investigating radical activities branded him "the most dangerous Negro in America," he just smiled and sat down at his old typewriter and started on another editorial blasting the system.

CHAPTER THREE

The Labor Movement

PHIL RANDOLPH didn't look or act the part of a man publicly labeled "the most dangerous Negro in America." He was no bomb-throwing revolutionary plotting guerrilla warfare, but to the established powers of his time, the ideas he printed in *The Messenger* were dynamite.

It was 1919. Randolph was thirty years old now, and had been married for four years. His wife, Lucille, was a handsome woman several years older. She had come to New York from Virginia, and soon was a successful businesswoman, first as a manager for a cosmetics firm and later as the owner of her own beauty parlor. Phil had met Lucille Green by chance—they worked for a time in the same building—and they hit it off immediately.

Phil was attracted by Lucille's charm and outgoing nature. She laughed easily and always seemed gay and full of fun. She loved parties and dancing, and was popular with her many friends. Phil, by contrast, was very serious, absorbed in his work and in the cause of socialism, and preferred to spend his evenings in reading or talking with friends about history, philosophy, and the black struggle for equality. The two complemented each other—Phil enjoyed Lucille's gaiety, and she admired his seriousness. Although many of their friends were surprised when they married, the couple lived happily for nearly fifty years until Mrs. Randolph's death in 1963.

Friends often visited their Harlem apartment for evenings of talk and relaxation, and they were frequent guests at the Dark Tower, the fashionable mansion of the black heiress A'Lelia Walker. Here the Randolphs would share ideas with the poets, artists, and novelists of the cultural movement, known as the Harlem Renaissance, who made the millionairess' townhouse their headquarters. The Randolphs acted too. Since they both shared a love for the works of Shakespeare—Phil had taken voice lessons from a Shakespearean actor—they joined a group of Harlem actors in staging plays for church and community groups.

Phil also enjoyed the theater and the vaudeville shows so popular at that time. But some theaters in Harlem would only allow black people to buy tickets for the balcony. Although many Negroes lived in Harlem, it was still a "white" area from 125th Street south, and many white-owned stores and theaters discriminated against black customers. So Phil devised a method of beating the system. He would enter the theater lobby, flatten himself against the wall next to the ticket office, slide his money across the open counter, and ask for orchestra seats. Sometimes it worked, but at other times the ticket-seller saw the brown hand and Phil had to take seats in the black section.

Lucille's store brought in enough money for them to live on. It had to, since *The Messenger* couldn't even pay its printing bills on time. Every now and then Phil would get onto the subway and travel to Brooklyn, where *The Messenger* was printed. There he would explain to the impatient printer that he had just forgotten his checkbook, and promised to pay the printing bill next week. And the printer, having heard the same story before, would just shrug his shoulders and wait.

Every so often Phil would sit at his desk in front of a pile of bills and wonder where they would get the money to continue publishing. But then a wealthy friend would donate a few hundred dollars or Chandler Owen would sell some advertising space, and the crisis would be over—until the next time. Luckily, he had a sense of humor, and could laugh in the face of difficulties.

Socialism wasn't making much headway either. The country had emerged from the war and from the "Red Summer" of 1919 in a state of exhaustion. Warren Harding was elected President in 1920 on a pledge of a "return to normalcy," and few people were interested in bold programs of social change.

But, with Chandler Owen, Phil organized an interracial organization, the Friends of Negro Freedom, to unionize migrant workers, help tenants, and educate black people to the benefits of Socialism. Often, Harlem-based members of the Friends would spend Sunday afternoons in their storefront office on 131st Street discussing social problems and planning their efforts to unionize black workers, but with the emergence of the Marcus Garvey movement, the group quickly became the major source of opposition to Garvey's Africa-based nationalism.

Marcus Garvey was a fiery orator from the Caribbean island of Jamaica who arrived in New York during

World War I and immediately started building a mass movement dedicated to African freedom and black separatism. Garvey wanted to establish a black empire in Africa that would inspire and protect black people everywhere.

Randolph and most other black leaders saw the Garvey movement as a threat to their efforts to win equal rights in America. They were alarmed by Garvey's willingness to compromise with the Ku Klux Klan and his rejection of social equality. His pride in his blackness seemed at times to be a kind of reverse racism, stirring enmity against white people. Randolph felt that Garvey didn't understand the economic basis of racism and the need to get black and white workers together to fight the system that oppressed them both. He scoffed at the Jamaican's ideas of empire. At a meeting in Harlem, Phil declared: "People are now fighting for the creation of democracies, not of empires. Negroes don't want to be the victims of black despotism any more than white despotism."

Garvey was riding high in the early 1920's. His mass parades and mass meetings caught Harlem's imagination, and millions of black people across the country joined his organization or sympathized with it. Phil campaigned hard against Garvey, and the pages of *The Messenger* were filled with warnings against the pan-Africanist's message. When Garvey got into trouble with the government because of some shady business dealings, Chandler Owen, supported by Randolph, helped pressure the government to prosecute him.

The battle against Garvey split the black community in two. One was either for Garvey or against him, and neither side would compromise with the other. One day, Phil got a package in the mail. When he opened it, he found the remains of a human hand, and a note threatening that if he did not stop agitating against Garvey, his hand would be mailed to someone else. The note was signed by the Ku Klux Klan, but Randolph was convinced that it was the work of fanatical Garveyites. He kept up his campaign until Garvey was jailed and then, in 1927, deported.

The Messenger was Phil's main forum for his attacks on Garvey, and for his attempt to spread Socialism among black people. The magazine sold about 45,000 copies each month and was well known and influential. Most black people at that time voted Republican, mainly because it was the party of Abraham Lincoln. However, largely through Phil's efforts, the Socialists started making inroads among black voters in Harlem. In the 1917 elections for mayor of New York City, Randolph and Owen campaigned actively for the Socialist candidate, Morris Hilquit. When the campaign dust had settled, Hilquit lost, as everyone knew he would. But, thanks to Randolph, he captured 25 percent of the black vote.

Three years later Phil entered politics as a candidate for office, running on the Socialist ticket for comptroller of the State of New York. Owen ran for the position of assemblyman from Harlem. Both lost, but the object of their campaigns was to educate voters to radical, new positions, and in that they were more successful. Phil ran unsuccessfully again in 1922, this time for the post of secretary of state of the State of New York.

He was also a lecturer at the Rand School of Social Science, and his deepening involvement in politics and social thought led to subtle shifts in his public positions. An indication of this was the change in *The Messenger*'s slogan from "The Only Radical Negro Magazine in

America," to "A Journal of Scientific Radicalism." Partly because of the success of *The Messenger,* it was no longer the only radical black magazine. Several others had cropped up, some of them more radical and revolutionary than *The Messenger* had become. Randolph and Owen felt that many of these publications were just explosions of anger in print and wanted to indicate through their new slogan that *The Messenger* stood for a scientific analysis of society's problems and for a radical solution to them.

Phil was still a militant fighter for equal rights, but the growth of the Garveyite movement and the growth of new groups on the extreme left, Communists and nationalist revolutionaries, made him seem more moderate. Where he had once welcomed the Communist revolution in Russia, he now warned against the manipulations of black American Communists.

Negro Communists are a menace [he wrote, who] break down the morals and confuse the aims of the New Negro Liberation Movement. So utterly senseless, unsound, unscientific, dangerous, and ridiculous are their policies and tactics that we are driven to conclude that they are either lunatics or agents provocateurs, stool pigeons of the United States Department of Justice. . . . Negro Communists seek to wreck all constructive, progressive, non-Communist programs.

By 1924 Randolph was considered one of the most influential black leaders in the country. That year he joined a delegation of black leaders and journalists to meet with President Coolidge to ask for a presidential pardon for some seventy of the black soldiers involved in the Houston riot of 1917 who · were still in federal prisons. Their fate was of great concern to the black community, since it was felt that the riots had been provoked by whites, and that many of the black soldiers had been jailed without receiving fair trials. The delegation handed the President a petition signed by 124,000 people asking for release of the prisoners, and some time later the soldiers were pardoned.

"For once we presented a solid united front," Randolph wrote in *The Messenger*. The bickering black leadership had stopped squabbling long enough to present a unified appeal on behalf of the black prisoners. While Phil recognized the differences between his own Socialist beliefs and the more conservative blacks who led the NAACP and other organizations, he understood that ideology should not stand in the way of fighting for black rights. By now it was apparent that neither his speeches and lectures nor his fiery *Messenger* editorials would turn the black masses to Socialism. He realized that it would be futile to limit himself to a single, narrow set of opinions. He believed, as ever, in the theories of Socialism, but he also believed in the practical task of winning greater progress for black people.

To Randolph, this meant putting less emphasis on the Socialist theories so close to his heart and more emphasis on organizing black workers and winning broader support among blacks who weren't much interested in Socialism or any other "ism." Once again, *The Messenger*'s masthead slogan changed. It no longer proclaimed itself "A Journal of Scientific Radicalism." Now it read: "The World's Greatest Negro Monthly."

In some ways, the magazine had not changed at all. It still struck a militant stance, although its anger had softened somewhat and was not as extreme as some of the new magazines put out by nationalist revolutionaries. Now there were occasional articles by black business leaders and others with whom Randolph did not necessarily agree. Capitalism, Garveyism, and the black Communists who danced to Moscow's tune were still enemies to be denounced regularly, but in somewhat less strident tones and alongside more articles dealing with the practical issues of struggling black workers.

Phil plunged into the task of organizing blacks into unions. He was still deeply suspicious of the dominant labor organization—the American Federation of Labor —but was anxious to cooperate with white unionists who would accept black workers as equals. In *The Messenger*'s early days, it bitterly attacked the AFL and Randolph supported its rival, the IWW. By the early 1920's the IWW had been almost destroyed by the arrest of its leaders, the growing conservatism of the country, and the failure of workers to support organizations that wanted to overthrow the system.

Randolph had condemned the AFL harshly. He believed that there could be no compromise with the capitalist system. He thought unions should be made up of all the workers in an industry, instead of just workers of a single craft or specialty, like carpenters or plumbers. And he hated the AFL's history of racial discrimination.

The dissolution of the American Federation of Labor [he wrote in *The Messenger*] would inure to the benefit of the labor movement in this country in particular and the international labor movement in general. It is organized upon unsound principles. It holds that there can be a partnership between labor and capital. . . . It stands for pure and simple unionism as against industrial unionism. . . . The present American Federation of Labor is the most wicked machine for the propagation of race prejudice in the country.

Strong words, but they were largely justified because of the historic discrimination against black workers. The rise of the labor movement was marked by forcing black workers out of jobs that had long been theirs. The poet and NAACP leader, James Weldon Johnson, recalled that in Jacksonville, Florida, at the time that Phil Randolph was growing up there:

All the most interesting things that came under my observation were being done by colored men. They drove the horse and mule teams, they built the houses, they laid the bricks, they painted the buildings and fences, they loaded and unloaded the ships. When I was a child, I did not know that there existed such a thing as a white carpenter or bricklayer or plasterer or tinner. The thought that white men might be able to load and unload the heavy drays or the big ships was too far removed from everyday life to enter my mind.

Now, few blacks were to be found in the occupations they had once dominated. As early as 1898 a writer for *The Atlantic Monthly* wrote of Washington, D.C., that:

At one period, some of the best buildings were constructed by colored workmen. Their employment in large numbers continued some time after the war. The British Legation, the Centre Market, the Freedmen's Bank, and at least four well-built school houses are monuments to the acceptability of their work under foremen of their own color. Today, apart from hod-carriers, not a colored workman is to be seen on new buildings, and a handful of jobbers and patchers, with possibly two carpenters who can undertake a large job, are all who remain of the body of colored carpenters and builders and stone cutters who were generally employed a quarter of a century ago.

In the years after its founding, in 1881, the AFL advocated a policy of non-discrimination. Since the AFL was a federation of many unions who controlled their own affairs, it could only enforce such policies by formulating rules that all members must follow. Many of its member unions were also fraternal organizations whose members joined not only for economic benefits, but also for social activities. Many white workers objected to allowing blacks to take part in these social functions as equals, even if they didn't object to working alongside them. Other white workers saw unions as a way to limit the numbers of qualified craftsmen and so to protect themselves from job competition.

The National Association of Machinists asked to become part of the AFL in 1890 and was refused because its constitution limited membership to white persons only. Samuel Gompers, then head of the AFL, made a personal appeal to the machinists to drop their constitutional bar against black workers. He believed that it was not fair to exclude blacks, and also that refusing to unionize black workers would play into the hands of employers by dividing the working class.

"Wage-workers," he wrote, "like many others, may not care to socially meet colored people, but as working men we are not justified in refusing them the right of the opportunity to organize for their common protection.

Then again, if organizations do, we will only make enemies of them, and of necessity they will be antagonistic to our interests."

Gompers saw clearly the need for black workers to belong to unions if they were to progress: "If the colored man is not permitted to organize, if he is not given the opportunity to protect and defend his interests, if a chance is not given him by which he could uplift his condition, the inevitable result must follow, that he will sink down lower and lower in his economic scale."

If Gompers and the other leaders of the AFL had stuck to their beliefs, things might have been different. But it was becoming clear to them that their principles of equal treatment for blacks were not shared by the bulk of their membership, and that many workers, especially in the South, would not join unions that also admitted blacks. Faced with a choice of sticking to their principles or abandoning them, and thus gaining new member unions, the AFL decided on a policy of racism.

The machinists were now allowed into the AFL. They dropped the "white only" clause from their constitution and, on Gompers' advice, shifted it to their entrance rituals. In that way, the Federation would not be embarrassed by their openly racist membership bars, while the union could continue to keep blacks out by more subtle means. Other unions entered the Federation in the same manner, with Gompers looking the other way as they continued to bar black workers from membership.

It was all part of the spirit of the age of Jim Crow. It was the time when segregated buses, drinking fountains, and other public facilities took root in the South and parts of the rest of the country. It was the time when black people were subjected to a growing list of restrictions. Now, in the late 1890's, the union movement became part of the racist web ensnaring black people.

By the beginning of the new century, the AFL was freely admitting unions with constitutional bars to black membership, and it now followed a policy of separating the races. Gompers still believed black workers should be organized, but now he backed a plan to organize black "federal" unions chartered directly by the central body of the Federation. Thus, if the plumbers' union, for example, refused to admit blacks, black plumbers could ask the AFL to give them a separate federal charter. In this way the AFL could enroll some blacks into unions without changing the racism of member unions. For the black worker, however, membership in a federal union brought very little. Such unions were weak, were answerable to white AFL officials, and were dominated by the local white union that originally refused to allow blacks as members and whose permission was necessary before a federal charter would be granted.

In 1902 W. E. B. Du Bois made a study of union membership and found that forty-three national unions had no black members and twenty-seven others had very few blacks. The only union that showed no signs of discrimination was the mine workers' union, whose twenty thousand black members amounted to more than half of all the blacks in the AFL.

Gompers was now catering to popular prejudices against black people. He declared that the AFL "does not necessarily proclaim that the social barriers which exist between the whites and blacks could or should be obliterated." He often claimed that white workers had more character and ambition than blacks. And he threatened "a race hatred far worse than any ever known," if black workers became strikebreakers.

Denied union membership, and thus the jobs in unionized trades, black workers ignored Gompers' threats and sometimes took the jobs of white workers who went on strike. This drove an even greater wedge between the races, since white workers saw blacks as a potential strikebreaking force that kept wages down, and blacks saw white workers as racists who kept them out of unions and jobs. Strikebreaking and union discrimination were behind some of the race riots of the period, such as the riot in East St. Louis in 1917 and the Chicago riot in 1919.

By the time Phil Randolph was bitterly denouncing the AFL in the pages of *The Messenger,* blacks were effectively shut out of almost all the craft unions. They were consistently paid far less than were unionized white workers, and were confined to laboring or industrial jobs. The Federation, with its philosophy of craft unionism, didn't bother trying to organize such jobs, and so neglected even larger numbers of black workers. It wasn't until the 1930's that large-scale unionization of industrial workers began.

So Randolph had ample reason to condemn the AFL, which he saw as the biggest barrier to black workers' chances for job opportunities. As his hopes for the growth of the IWW faded, he turned to developing independent unions made up of black workers, and to cooperation with those few union leaders who rejected the AFL's official policies of discrimination.

Early in 1919 he became one of the founders of a new organization called the National Association for the Promotion of Labor Unionism Among Negroes. Chandler Owen was president, Randolph served as secretary-treasurer, and its advisory board was made up of a number of prominent Socialist politicians and labor leaders. The group's emblem was a circle within which a black hand and a white hand were clasped. Its slogan was "Black and White Workers Unite." The group mounted an attempt to organize black laundry workers, and to form a branch of the bakers' union made up of black bakers. Neither effort was successful and the organization folded.

The next year, Randolph and Owen were elected to the executive council of the National Brotherhood Workers of America, an all-black union with considerable strength among black shipyard workers in Virginia. The union's organizers considered themselves "militant revolutionaries," and were inspired by *The Messenger.* Their goal was to organize black workers in all industries and in agriculture. For a while *The Messenger* served as the Brotherhood's regular magazine, and Randolph and Owen played a major role in the organization.

But this venture too ended in failure. The far stronger white longshoremen's union signed up many black workers, cutting down on the Brotherhood's strength, and an economic slowdown in the Virginia dockyards put other blacks out of work. Since the main source of the organization's membership came from that region, the Brotherhood soon found itself in serious financial trouble. Somehow it expected *The Messenger,* itself always in debt, to come up with needed cash and, when it didn't, Randolph and Owen were asked to resign. The Brotherhood itself died in 1921.

Randolph had learned much from these experiences.

By the 1920's he was more convinced than ever that the black man's best hope lay in organized labor. He recognized the open discrimination of the AFL's leadership, but he also saw that some unions would cooperate in organizing black workers. His hopes for a Socialist revolution were unrealistic, and he now believed the only way to bring about Socialism in the years ahead was to develop a strong labor movement in which blacks had their fair share of the jobs and union memberships.

While his many efforts to organize black workers had ended in failure, Phil had established a good reputation among many of them who believed, as he did, in the potential power of unions. He was known to be honest and to be willing to make sacrifices for the cause of labor democracy. So when a handful of train porters thought of a way to start a union of their own, they quite naturally turned to Randolph for help. In doing so, they changed their own lives, put Phil Randolph on the path of fame and national leadership, and helped to change the course of American history.

CHAPTER FOUR

Struggle for a Black Union

TODAY, jet planes streak across the country linking the coasts in several hours' flying time. On the ground, rail tracks crisscross the land, but the great days of railroading are dead. The famous trains that once represented the height of luxury travel are no more. Travelers prefer the speed of planes or the mobility of their own cars, and even the grain and freight shipments that were once the backbone of railroading's prosperity are now shared with trucks and jet cargo planes.

In the 1920's there was no great network of highways slicing the landscape, and the airplanes were still flimsy two-seaters incapable of carrying passengers. If you wanted to travel anywhere, you took a train, and if your journey meant night travel—and you could afford it— you would take a Pullman sleeping car.

By day, the cars of the Pullman Company looked like any other cars of a passenger train. But by night, the seats folded over, berths were lowered from the top of the car, and it was converted into a room of double-decker beds on either side of a center aisle. The men who converted the daytime sitting car into the nighttime sleeping berths, who made the beds and attended to the passengers' needs, were the porters.

Pullman porters were black—all of them. It was a company policy, started with its first sleeping car just after the Civil War. Black workers were cheap, and after slavery ended there was a plentiful supply of such workers. Also, the Pullman Company reasoned, blacks were servile, used to giving personal service to white people. The humble, bowing porter, his faced creased by a wide, white-toothed smile, would give the traveler a feeling of luxury and personal attention. And to ensure that those smiles would be plentiful and the service cheerful, the company paid its porters very low wages to keep them dependent upon tips from the passengers.

At first, the black porters accepted their lot. The work was preferable to long hours of backbreaking labor in the fields of the South. Even the low wages, when combined with the tips, weren't so bad compared with what other black workers were making. And at a time when few black people traveled more than a few miles from the rural farms on which they were born, the Pullman porter had great prestige in his community. He not only traveled beyond the imaginings of many of his neighbors, he also associated, although in the role of servant, with wealthy white people.

The gratitude of newly freed ex-slaves soon wore off, and by the turn of the century many porters were dissatisfied with their low pay and poor working conditions. In 1909 some porters tried to start a union, but they were defeated by the company's opposition and by the fear and apathy of their fellow porters. Another effort in 1913 was crushed when the organizers were fired. Two other attempts crumbled when the company fired the ringleaders and threatened any who joined a union with the same fate.

Like many big companies of the day, the Pullman Company would not deal with a union. Pullman's policy was briefly and brutally summarized by a special commission that investigated the bitter 1893 strike at the company's car-building plant:

> The Company does not recognize that labor organizations have any place or necessity in Pullman, where the Company fixes wages and rents and refuses to treat with labor organizations. The laborer can work or quit on the terms offered; that is the limit of his rights. To join a labor organization in order to secure the protection of union against wrongs, real or imaginary, is overstepping the limits and arouses hostility. This position secures all the advantages of the concentration of capital, ability, power, and control for the Company in its labor dealings and deprives the employees of any such advantages or protection as a labor union might afford. In this respect the Pullman company is behind the age.

And during World War I a U.S. Senate committee reported: "The employees of the Pullman Co. are unable to improve their conditions through organization . . . workers known to be members of labor unions are promptly discharged." It was also noted that "a system of espionage caused black workers to be fearful of affiliating with unions of any sort."

The porters were at the mercy of the company. It was obvious that it would never deal with a union of black porters whom it saw as grinning servants and not as men and equals. Not even organized labor would help the porters. The major railroad unions refused to admit any blacks, and they even used their power to get Congress to exclude Pullman car workers from the protection of laws regulating railroads and their employees.

To meet the growing restlessness among its porters, the company organized an Employee Representation Plan in 1920. This was a "company union" dominated by Pullman executives and their stooges among the porters. There was also a Pullman Porters Benefit Association financed partly by the company and partly by monthly payments from the porters. This served as a social and insurance group, paying small sickness and death benefits in return for dues of $26 a year. By forming these organizations, the company gave many porters the impression of fairness, thus helping to prevent the militants among them from starting a real union and fighting for real benefits.

In the summer of 1925 Phil Randolph became interested in the plight of the porters. A number of militant porters who were regular readers of *The Messenger* appealed to him for help. Phil investigated the situation and began a series of articles on the callous treatment of the porters by the Pullman Company. What the porters need, Randolph wrote, is a union that "could sit around a table and bargain collectively, with the power of a work stoppage to back them up."

Several porters who had tried, unsuccessfully, to start just such a union in the past, agreed. But they knew that any attempt to organize their fellow workers would lead to dismissal from their jobs and that other porters would be terrorized into rejecting a union. If a successful organizing drive was to be mounted, it would have to be led by someone from the outside, someone who didn't depend on the company for his livelihood.

Phil Randolph was their man. His articles had created a stir among the porters. *The Messenger* was passed from hand to hand in railroad trains from New York to California. Heads nodded in agreement with his strong words and plans of action. "Someone ought to do something," porters murmured.

A group of New York porters, led by Ashley Totten, W. H. Des Verney, and William Bowe invited Randolph to speak privately with them. They met at Des Verney's home and, after a lengthy discussion on the ways in which the porters could be helped, asked him to lead them in a new union.

Phil was stunned and tried to stall for time. "I am not sure that I had ever seen a Pullman car then—much less ridden in one," he later recalled.

The task was enormous. There were ten thousand porters spread thinly across the vast spaces of the continent. Most were apathetic and fearful of any activity that would annoy the company. They knew that jobs were scarce and even if a porter's job paid poorly, they might not find work elsewhere. Organizing a union takes money, lots of it. The workers were poor and Phil was broke. Finally, with the Pullman Company, the would-be union was taking on one of the richest, most powerful, and most ruthless of America's giant corporations. The prospects for success were dim indeed.

But Phil wasn't one to shirk from trying the impossible. He had devoted most of his adult years to fighting for his dream of a better society, and now he was prepared for his greatest battle. "I'll do it," he told his porter friends, and they immediately plunged into the task of building a union.

The Brotherhood of Sleeping Car Porters was born on a hot, murky night in August 1925 at a meeting of fifty porters in Harlem's Elks Hall. Phil strode to the podium and told the audience that they could not be sure that company spies weren't present. He explained that if stool pigeons reported that porters took part in an organizing meeting, they'd be fired the next day. "So I don't want anyone to say a word," he told them. "That way this will be my own meeting and you won't be in danger from the company."

"I said to them," Randolph recalled, "that I was going to give the invocation, and I gave it; that I was going to make all the announcements, and I made them; that I was going to introduce the speaker, which I did; and that I was going to speak, and I did speak. And after I finished speaking," he went on, "I said the benediction and then told the men to go home and not stand around on street corners talking about the meeting because if they did they would be reported in the morning. In fact, they might be reported anyway, simply because they had attended the meeting, even though they did not actually take part in any of the proceedings."

He made all the motions, seconded all the motions, and ran a one-man show. It was unusual, but necessary. Within hours, the company was alerted by its spies and began to question porters who had attended.

Ashley Totten was fired for his role in starting the Brotherhood; he became an officer of the union. W. H. Des Verney quit his job to work for the union, although it meant giving up his right to the pension he was entitled to for his thirty-seven years as a porter. Randolph might have been thinking of these determined men when he later said: "We had militant, aggressive men who were willing to go without bread for the victory of their union —and they did go without bread, too."

The new union's first task was to recruit members. This was difficult. Company spies were everywhere, and the suspicion that a porter was active in union activities would get him fired immediately. Many porters were aware of the discrimination by white unions and were suspicious of any labor organization. They might not like what the company was doing to them, but at least they knew Pullman and its rules—and they didn't know what, if anything, they'd gain from joining the union.

Two hundred porters joined almost immediately. They were to be the activist core of the union. The rest would have to be convinced by a network of Brotherhood offices wherever there were large numbers of porters, and by personal organizing trips on the part of Randolph, Totten, Des Verney, and others. An office was set up in Chicago, the Pullman Company's headquarters, under the direction of Milton P. Webster, a former porter who had been fired for his union activities years before. C. L. Dellums, a California porter who was later to become the Brotherhood's president, was put in charge of recruiting members on the West Coast.

While Frank Crosswaith, a prominent Harlem Socialist and labor organizer helped out in the New York office, Randolph set up labor institutes and labor conferences in big cities from coast to coast, explaining the program of the Brotherhood and the need for workers to organize. After each meeting a collection plate was passed around so Randolph and other Brotherhood officials could buy a ticket to their next city. Often, Randolph was stranded for days until he could raise the fare to return to New York.

The Brotherhood's main office was the two rooms on Seventh Avenue that already served as *The Messenger*'s office. Pullman porters who lived in Harlem learned not to walk on that street for fear that company spies would see them and think they were officers in the Brotherhood. *The Messenger* itself sprouted a new slogan on its masthead. "The Official Organ of the Brotherhood of Sleeping Car Porters," it proudly proclaimed.

Now, with a union officially started and with a publicity organ, Randolph had to get the porters' grievances before the company and the public. Wages and hours were the prime source of complaint, but working conditions were so bad and company regulations made a porter's life so difficult that the union's list of demands was a long one.

The first demand was recognition of the union. It wanted the company to officially recognize the Brotherhood as the representative of the porters and to sign a contract with it, legally agreeing to terms of payment, working conditions, and machinery to settle differences peaceably.

The union asked for a minimum wage of $150 per month, more than double the measly $67.50 the Pullman Company paid the average porter. And it wanted shorter hours. Porters worked 300 to 400 hours per month. This meant that they had to endure a 100-hour week, or about two-and-a-half times as many hours as the average workweek today. The Brotherhood also pointed out that porters weren't paid for time spent preparing the cars before the trains left the station, nor for cleaning them up after passengers arrived at their destination.

Another of the union's demands demonstrated the ex-

hausting nature of a porter's job. It insisted that porters
be allowed four hours of sleep on the first night of a run
and six hours on following nights. Since a porter was
supposed to be at the passengers' beck and call at every
moment, the company didn't allow for sleeping on the
job. A porter was permitted just three hours of sleep on
the first night of a train's journey, none on the second
and third nights. On the fourth night he got just three
hours. The popular stereotype of the Pullman porter
shuffling slowly down the aisle of his car, head bent low,
was, Randolph charged, due to the fact that the poor man
was exhausted and bone-tired from lack of sleep.

Out of his meager salary and the uncertain tips, the
porter was expected to buy his own uniform, his own
meals, and the polish and brushes with which he shined
passengers' shoes. He was also accountable for the ash-
trays, towels, sheets, and blankets in the car. When a
passenger walked off with one of these as a "souvenir" of
his trip, it was the porter who had to pay for it.

On and on the list of grievances went. Porters weren't
paid for extra time when their trains were late or delayed; they often had to do the conductor's job in addition to their own without getting adequate extra pay;
they often completed a long run only to be ordered out
immediately on another train; and they sometimes were
required to report to the Pullman office where they
would wait all day to be assigned to a train, only to be
sent home without pay for their waiting time.

Finally, the porters wanted a real pension plan. At the
time, the company paid a pension of a paltry $18 per
month to porters who retired at the age of seventy after
working a minimum of twenty years. And the porters had
no right to this pension; the company claimed that it

could stop payment "for any reason at any time." One of
the reasons it used to cut off pensions from retired porters
was union activity. A retired West Coast porter, "Dad"
Moore, told the company to keep its pension and went to
work for the union. Other retired porters did valuable
work in spreading the union's message but had to keep it
secret for fear of losing the little income they had in their
old age.

And so the long, hard work of building a union was
begun. The company, as expected, ignored the porters'
demands and refused to meet with Randolph or the other
leaders of the Brotherhood. But more and more porters
were flocking to the union's banner, often signing up
secretly.

As he went around the country speaking to meetings of
porters and their friends, Randolph would denounce the
company union: "An organization that is handed down
by the boss to the wage earner is for the benefit of the
boss and not the wage earner."

And to the public, which was watching the struggle
between a union of poor black workers and a giant
corporation, Randolph pointed out:

"You no longer have the wooden car, no longer have
you the typical porter. That porter has passed and a new
porter has come into being. He is urbanized; he is indus-
trialized, subject to this standardized civilization, and he
is thinking through this new medium and it is organized
labor."

Randolph saw the struggling little union as a symbol of
the black man's determination to achieve a greater measure of dignity, self-respect, and organized power. Black
people had, he wrote, "reached the point in their development . . . where they will act deliberately, so-

berly, coolly, and dispassionately to adopt the course of action which is calculated to protect and advance their social, economic, and political interests."

So there was a lot at stake as the young union squared off against the powerful corporation in a struggle that would last a dozen years.

CHAPTER FIVE

The Battle with Pullman

THE Pullman Company fought back with everything it had. First it tried a "soft" line to convince porters and the black community that it was their friend. But behind this velvet-glove approach was the clenched fist of repression.

Shortly after the Brotherhood was started, the company grandly announced that it would institute an employee stock-purchase plan. A Pullman worker would be allowed to buy one share of stock—priced at $140—for every $500 earned in salary. Just how porters, whose wages averaged under $1,000 a year, could afford to take advantage of this plan was never explained.

Then the company raised wages by 8 percent, far less than the Brotherhood demanded but enough, company officials thought, to satisfy the men. There were plenty of porters who were grateful for any scrap the company threw them. Randolph hit hard at this kind of thinking in the pages of *The Messenger*. "There are too many Uncle Toms in the service," he wrote. "These old-fashioned Negroes do not want to improve their positions.

With their slave-thinking they bow and lick the boots of company officials who either feel sorry for them or hate them."

The company also tried to win blacks in its fight against the union by picturing itself as a friend of the race through its employment of Negroes. In addition to the ten thousand porters, it also employed six thousand other blacks in its car-building shops and other positions. It said that by employing only blacks as porters, it gave black people a monopoly in that job, safe from the inroads of competition from white workers.

It even tried to win support by publicizing the fact that Robert T. Lincoln, the son of President Lincoln, was a former president of the company and continued to serve on its board of directors. But this Lincoln was known for his anti-Negro views and Randolph mocked the company's attempt to sentimentally appeal to blacks' hero-worship of the President who signed the Emancipation Proclamation. The son, Randolph charged, "has bent his influence and name to the notorious exploitation of Negroes as *Pullman slaves.*"

Randolph also attacked the company's stepped-up program of social programs, such as dances, for its workers. "If by giving them a band," he wrote, "the company can get their feet more active in dancing than their heads in thinking, the company will certainly give them bands."

The company showed a tougher side in its battle with the union. Members were fired or transferred to less desirable runs. Inspectors rode trains that had union porters and invented charges of broken company rules that led to firings. Soon, an atmosphere of fear was created and the union was forced deeper underground.

A key element in the company's fight against the

Brotherhood was its system of welfare workers. These were men supposedly hired to help Pullman employees who had problems or needed advice and assistance. But their real function was to control the workers, serving as spies for the company and influencing porters not to join the union. The men called them "stool pigeons," and Randolph rightly said that "porters have too much sense to listen to the advice of someone who is paid $150 a month to make them satisfied with $67.50."

After months of pressure failed to stem the tide of porters rushing to the union's support, the company stepped up its policy of firing militant workers. More than five hundred men lost their jobs during the long struggle for union recognition. Many of these were replaced by Mexicans or Filipinos, as the company tried to demonstrate that there were other minorities in the country who needed work and who might be expected to be more grateful than the black porters.

Pullman recognized that Randolph was the key to the union's success. If they could eliminate him, the union was bound to fold, just as earlier attempts to organize had failed. So they launched a tremendous campaign against Randolph, accusing him of just about everything they could think of that would damage his reputation.

Randolph, it charged, was a Communist, an atheist, and a revolutionary. He wanted blacks to control and dominate white people. He was a traitor who fought the country in World War I and was a slacker who refused to be drafted. And he was an "outside agitator" disturbing the peace and harmony enjoyed by the porters and their benevolent employers. In short, Phil Randolph was a monster and no one could sleep in safety while he was at large.

These attacks on his character were ridiculous, but they forced Randolph on the defensive. He had to explain all over again that he wasn't a Communist, indeed was fighting to keep Communists out of the Brotherhood. He had to once more defend his record of moral objection to the war, and his belief in racial justice and equality, with no one race dominating the others. As to his being an "outside agitator," Phil pointed out that the porters asked him to organize them and he wrote that "of course labor leaders are 'outsiders' and if they were not 'outsiders' they would be as soon as the capitalists learned their identity. . . . When unable to break up a union, American capitalists invariably seek to eliminate the leader of the union."

In meeting after meeting, all over the country, he told porters:

Brothers . . . when I enlisted in the cause, I knew that slanderers would attempt to blacken my character with infamy. I knew that among the wicked, corrupt, and unenlightened my pleadings would be received with disdain and reproach; that persecution would assail me on every side; that the dagger of the assassin would gleam behind my back; that the arm of arrogant power would be raised to crush me to the earth; that I would be branded as a disturber of peace, as a madman, fanatic, an incendiary, a Communist, anarchist, and whatnot; that the heel of friendship would be lifted against me; that love would be turned into hatred; confidence into suspicion, respect into derision; that my worldly interests would be jeopardized. I knew that the base and servile would accuse me of being actuated with the hope of reward. But, Brethren, I am undaunted and unafraid. The only reward that I seek is that your cause secures a full and complete vindication. Despite the curses that have been heaped upon

my head because I dared to tell the truth, I have no ill feeling
against any man. Let us not hate our detractors, for they must
be saved with the expansive and redeeming love of the
Brotherhood.

There rarely was a dry eye in the house when he
finished, and as the company's attacks mounted, the
porters drew closer to the man who was giving his all in
their name and for their cause.

Attacks on Randolph and the Brotherhood also came
from black politicians, church leaders, and newspapers.
Many of these felt, as a resolution passed by the national
convention of the Elks, a powerful black fraternal organization, put it: "unionism is calculated to do our people
all sorts of harm and injure them with the employing class
in America . . . it [should] be the continued policy of
our people everywhere to line up with the best class of
American citizenship, which . . . constitute the large
employers of labor."

But such expressions of traditional anti-unionism were
also joined by attacks bankrolled by the company. One
black politician who attacked the Brotherhood's leaders
as "professional agitators whose motives . . . are self-
seeking and sinister" was exposed as having received
$4,000 from the Pullman Company.

Some churches supported the union, letting it use their
auditoriums for meetings, and helping it to raise money
and to acquaint the public with its cause. But other
ministers denounced the union from their pulpit, often
out of fear of alienating local business leaders who were
anti-labor, and sometimes in exchange for donations
from the same sources. One preacher opened his church

to the union after angrily refusing a bribe of $300 to refuse it a meeting space.

The Negro press, which should have spread the Brotherhood's message, was largely anti-union. The reason was easy to determine. Often, readers would find anti-Brotherhood editorials next to costly full-page advertisements of the Pullman Company. Fighting back, Randolph ran a series of articles in *The Messenger* showing how the black press had been bought by the Pullman interests. He branded the popular Chicago *Defender,* the Chicago *Surrender,* and called it the "World's Greatest Weakly." Another newspaper, the Chicago *Whip,* was revealed to be owned by lawyers who represented the Pullman Company.

Some black papers were objective, and others were squarely behind the union, especially after it urged blacks not to buy newspapers that supported the company against the porters. The *Defender* switched sides in late 1928, suddenly calling Randolph "brilliant and fearless," and as the fight wore on, other papers backed the Brotherhood.

The battle for the union was becoming a battle for the minds of black people. Randolph no longer spoke of Socialism or of the natural enmity between capitalists and workers. He knew that black people, despite the ravages and exploitations of the economic system, were not radical and would not support a Socialist movement. So he stressed the accepted principles of unionism and the justice of the porters' cause.

"This movement is not radical," he wrote, "except in the sense that the whole trade union movement is fundamentally radical. . . . The porters also want a voice in the determination of the conditions under which they work, the abolition of the Pullman feudalistic paternalism, a relic of the old master-slave relationship. They want to maintain their manhood, their self-respect."

Because most porters, along with the bulk of the black community, were deeply religious, his writings and speeches were rich in Biblical references although he had long abandoned the faith of his father. Brotherhood pamphlets and announcements were always headed: "Ye Shall Know the Truth and the Truth Shall Set You Free." And he tried to enlist the church in labor's cause, saying: "The Negro Church, representing the working-class population, can serve the race nobly in championing the cause of labor and yet remain true to its traditions, since Jesus Christ was a carpenter and all of his disciples workmen."

His speeches would usually end with lines such as: "Stand upon Thy Feet and the God of Truth and Justice and Victory Will Speak to Thee." The many hours he spent at his father's feet in small country churches were now being put to a more worldly purpose.

Such religious appeals deepened support for the porters and for Randolph's growing role as a folk-hero. He became known as a "Moses leading his people from the land of bondage," and as "St. Philip of the Pullman Porters." To the working men of the union, though, he was simply, the "Chief," the affectionate nickname that has remained.

Randolph saw the struggle for the union as an important weapon to instill racial pride and a positive racial consciousness among black people who had been psychologically damaged by the racism of their society. At a time when black meant inferior, Phil Randolph was telling the humblest of black workingmen that they too were important, that they too were of value, and that they too were the equals of anyone else.

"Brotherhood members," he often said, "are a crucial challenge to the Nordic creed of white superiority, for only white men are supposed to organize for power, for justice, and for freedom." He tried to give the porters and their friends in the black community the feeling that the white majority was impressed by their courageous stand in the face of a powerful company. "The Pullman Company and White America are amazed, surprised, and dumbfounded at your manly, militant, clean, courageous, and consistent fight for justice," he declared.

He was right. The Brotherhood's battle was coming to the attention of the white press, and it was generally recognized that the porters were fighting for more than higher pay and shorter hours. As *The Nation* editorialized, "These men who punch our pillows and shine our shoes and stow our bags under the seat bear in their black hands no little responsibility for the industrial future of the race."

The Brotherhood's first goals had been reached. By the end of 1927, after just two years of existence, it claimed more than seven thousand members. Just about every train steaming up and down the West Coast was manned by Brotherhood porters, and a thumping majority of trains outside the South were staffed by union men. The period Randolph had described as "watchful waiting" marked by the slogan "To Make Haste Slowly," was at an end. The time had come to press the fight on a higher level.

The Pullman Company refused to meet with Brotherhood leaders. It didn't accept their calls and left their

letters unanswered. Under the law regulating railroad
labor relations, unions claiming to represent workers
could ask the government to intervene in a dispute with
employers. Since Pullman wouldn't deal with the union,
Randolph decided, maybe the government would force
them to, and he took the case to the Mediation Board.

The company resisted, saying that there was nothing to
negotiate since it "knew of no dispute between itself and
its porters." It claimed that its own company union ade-
quately represented its workers and tried to prove this by
showing that the vast majority of employees belonged to
it. But the Brotherhood quickly submitted more than a
thousand statements from porters saying they joined the
company's union because they were afraid they'd be fired
if they didn't. Randolph also proved that the majority of
Pullman's porters were Brotherhood members.

In the summer of 1927 the union won its first victory.
The board ruled that the Brotherhood *did* represent the
majority of the workers and suggested that Pullman and
the union submit their dispute to an independent arbitrator who would weigh the facts and make decisions
both sides would have to follow.

This was what Randolph was hoping for. But the
company wasn't going to give up so easily. Arbitration
was a voluntary step, and Pullman wasn't about to vol-
unteer. It feared that the arbitrator would decide that
the Brotherhood was the rightful representative of the
porters. That would mean the end of the company union
and force the company to deal with the Brotherhood.

Meanwhile, Randolph tried to put pressure on the
company in another way. Pullman justified its low wages
on the grounds that porters received tips. But Randolph
wanted the company to pay a living wage; porters should

not depend on tips to make ends meet. He charged that tipping was an evil practice that subsidized the company, enabling it to pay low wages. "We are not servile beggars who stand hat in hand for a few coins," he thundered. "We are men who want to be paid like men for a man's work."

He took this argument to the Interstate Commerce Commission, the federal agency that regulates business transactions across state lines. There the Brotherhood argued that tipping was a violation of the law because when a passenger bought a ticket, he was entitled to full services without paying anything extra, such as a tip to the porter.

But the commission ruled that it had no jurisdiction over the dispute between the Brotherhood and the company because it was essentially a labor dispute over wages. Randolph probably expected such a decision, but he also knew that the publicity value of the case would be effective. It was.

Public support for the porters grew, especially when Randolph pointed out that the amount the riding public spent in tips was more than the company's dividends to its stockholders. The public, by tipping porters, he argued, was enabling the company to pay fat dividends. Many people agreed with the popular journalist, Heywood Broun, who wrote: "The Pullman Company is a panhandler. . . . I'm tired of tipping the Pullman Company."

The fight against tipping was more than a nuisance attack on the company. Randolph believed that there could be no real dignity to labor if it depended on tips. If the porters had won, American life might have been drastically changed for barbers, waiters, and other workmen who depended on tips to supplement their low wages. And for black workers, Randolph's fight against tipping was a call to dignity and a public demonstration that blacks were not a servant class but were proud working people who wanted wages, not tips.

By the beginning of 1928, with the company still refusing to deal with the Brotherhood, Phil Randolph took his case to the White House. Joined by other black leaders, he met in January with President Calvin Coolidge.

They made a strange pair, the Socialist union leader, who less than a decade before had been branded the "most dangerous Negro in America," and the President who had made his national reputation as a union-busting anti-labor mayor of Boston. As Randolph spoke in those deep, slow tones that had echoed in so many ghetto street-corner and church meetings, the President sat tight-lipped, nodding his head occasionally, but barely speaking. He was aptly known as "Silent Cal."

Randolph opened the discussion by telling the President about the low wages and bad working conditions of the porters. He explained why they banded together in a union to fight for their rights, and he told of his fruitless efforts to meet with company officials.

Mr. President, I am here to tell you that the company has refused to enter arbitration as recommended by your Mediation Board. That means my union will have to call a strike. If we strike, there will be a national emergency on the railroads, and under the law the Mediation Board will have to refer the matter to you.

Because you may find yourself in the position of having to take action at that time, I wanted to let you know what the facts are, and what my union is trying to accomplish. I want you to have all the facts so that you can make your decision.

Coolidge thanked Randolph for coming but said nothing. They smiled, shook hands, and the black delegation left the President's office. Back in New York, Randolph met with the Brotherhood's officers. "I don't know what Coolidge will do, but we've got to go ahead and call a strike vote. It's our only chance to force the company to deal with us," he said.

This was a crucial moment for the young union. Many porters had joined the Brotherhood in the face of company reprisals. They had stuck it out for nearly three years. But a strike meant walking off their jobs and going without pay for weeks, perhaps months. Today, large unions have strike funds out of which they give striking members at least some money. But the struggling young Brotherhood could barely pay its electric bills, much less help support its members. Porters wondered: What if the company just hired strikebreakers and we never get our jobs back? There were plenty of people out of work; plenty of people to take the places of striking porters. Fear spread through the ranks.

Randolph had to quiet their fears. He had to explain that voting for a strike didn't mean a strike had to take place; it merely gave the union's leaders the right to call a strike. It was a powerful weapon, intended to force a company to bargain.

He explained how, just a few weeks before, one of the railroad unions had voted for a strike and the Mediation Board stepped in and settled the dispute. Clearly, that was his strategy—not to force the men to endure the hardship of a strike, but to force government action that would make the Pullman Company deal with the Brotherhood.

The porters still believed in Phil Randolph. The strike vote was taken in April 1928. Only seventeen votes were against it, but more than six thousand porters voted in favor. Armed with this vote of confidence, Randolph set June 8 as the date the strike would start. "If the company refuses to deal with us by then," he told reporters, "every Pullman porter in the country will walk off his job and the trains will not run." People will realize, he said, "that this is a new Pullman porter and he represents the spirit of the New Negro."

The fight was back in the hands of the Mediation Board. Under the law, it could advise the President that the strike threat was an emergency and that he should appoint an official board to investigate the situation and recommend solutions. The Mediation Board stalled. Finally, just before the strike was to start, it announced its verdict. No emergency exists, it said. A strike would not cause a transportation crisis. It would not recommend any action by the President.

Randolph was stunned. He rushed to Washington to meet with members of the board. "How could you rule this way?" he asked them. "When only six hundred members of another union voted to strike against one railroad, you declared an emergency. But we are seven thousand strong and our strike will affect people all over the nation." The board hemmed and hawed. Slowly the picture became clear: in previous cases the railroad had asked that the strike be prevented. It was apparent that the board, like other government agencies, was there to protect the employers, not the workers.

The long hand of the Pullman Company was obviously at work. Randolph left the meeting convinced that the company had persuaded the board, and "perhaps the President himself," that if it declared an emergency and allowed this small union of black workers to defy a giant corporation, "it was going to stir up the Negroes of this country and make them cocky, so that they would feel their power and that this would cause the business interests to have trouble with their Negro workers."

So the fight for government intervention was lost. The battleground was cleared for a fight to the finish between the company and the union, and the odds were all in the company's favor. Having come so close to victory, the Brotherhood was face to face with disaster.

CHAPTER SIX

Black Labor Power

To strike or not to strike. That was the big question facing Randolph and the Brotherhood's leaders. They had thought that the mere threat of a strike would bring government action. Their gamble failed, and now they were faced with a painful decision that would hurt the union, no matter what course they took. A strike would be long and would bring great hardship to the porters. But failure to strike would be a public confession of the Brotherhood's weakness, and might even kill the union completely.

Randolph knew that if the porters went on strike, they would need allies. He traveled to Washington to meet with the current president of the AFL, William Green. Green had helped the Brotherhood in the past, and now he could give advice on what the union's next step should be. And if they decided to strike, it was Green and the AFL whose support was crucial.

Randolph brought Green up to date on the situation. "The company is ready to withstand a long strike," he said. "They have gathered a large group of strikebreakers who will step into the porters' jobs as soon as a strike is called. Pullman has arranged to have these men sleep and eat near the railroad yards, ready to work at a moment's notice. They've got extra police ready to move into the stations and rail terminals in case of a strike."

"How about your men?" Green asked. "Will they walk off the job if the Brotherhood calls a strike?"

"I don't know," Randolph answered. "I get the feeling that they never really believed it would come to such a drastic step. They are poor people who are afraid of losing their jobs, no matter how badly they're treated. Also, the company has frightened them. Before a porter leaves on a train, Pullman supervisors ask him whether he'll go on strike, and of course he answers 'no' because he's afraid of being fired."

Green pondered what Randolph told him. He leaned forward and said grimly: "Phil, I'm afraid a strike would fail. The employment situation is very bad these days. Many people are out of work, especially Negroes. The company would find it very easy to replace Brotherhood men on the trains.

"There's something else you should know," he went on. "The public isn't ready to accept a strike by Negroes. The public doesn't like strikes, and it is necessary to have public support for a strike to succeed. In your case, the strikers would be Negroes and, let's face the truth, the public sees Negroes as a submarginal group of workers who should 'know their place.' The only way you could win a strike is if the public refused to ride Pullman trains, and that won't happen."

Randolph stiffened in his chair, waiting for Green to deliver the final blow. "A strike at this time would play

into the hands of the Pullman Company," the AFL
leader said. "It is my firm conviction that the best interests of all workers concerned would be served through
the postponement of strike action and the substitution of a
campaign of education and public enlightenment regard-
ing the justice of your case and the seriousness of your
grievances."

Randolph returned to New York with a heavy heart.
He called the Brotherhood leadership together to hear
the bad news. "A strike would fail," he told them. "Mr.
Green told the truth, and bitter as it is, we must recognize the truth of our situation." The others agreed. They
had been talking with porters every day, and knew of
their fears. If a strike was called, many porters would stay
on the job. Besides, the union's treasury was empty. It
couldn't possibly win a power struggle with the company
if it struck.

In his public statements, Randolph tried to make the
Brotherhood's failure to call the strike it had threatened
seem a victory. "We know the plans of the company now
to break our strike," he said, "and we can overcome them
when we stage our strike later on. The strike is merely
postponed. Meanwhile, we have forced the company to
spend a million dollars to prepare for a strike, thus doing
it as much damage as if a strike were actually called."

But such statements fooled no one. The Brotherhood's
failure to actually strike showed just how weak it was in
relation to the company. Bleak days lay ahead.

The immediate effect of calling off the strike was the
loss of faith in the union by many porters. They weren't
ready to strike, and now they saw the uselessness of
pretending to do battle with Pullman. The Brotherhood
had shown how weak it was, and many porters were

afraid to be labeled "union men" by the company, so
they dropped out. Members stopped paying their dues
and coming to meetings. "Yes, we need the union," one
porter said, "but the company is just too strong for us.
It's no use."

Within months, the more than seven thousand
Brotherhood members dwindled to less than twenty-five
hundred. The company, sniffing victory, delivered another blow aimed at Randolph. "If this known Socialist,
and an outsider," were removed from the Brotherhood's
leadership, it said, perhaps some agreement could be
reached. It was an attempt to split the porters who remained loyal to the Brotherhood by breaking the union
into two groups—Randolph and his followers versus
those who would be willing to dump Randolph and reach
any agreement with the company at any price. The union
saw through this trick. It knew that Randolph had dedicated himself to the cause of the porters, going without
salary and without rest. It gave the company a firm "no."

The winter of 1928–29 was a cold one. The Brotherhood's membership was down to a hard core of followers.
It owed money for its rent. The telephones and elec-
tricity were shut off because it couldn't pay the bills.
Even *The Messenger* was gone. After more than ten
years, Randolph had to end his magazine, for there was
no money left to pay its bills. Mrs. Randolph's income
from her beauty shop supported them, for Phil refused to
accept a salary from the union. Several organizers had to
leave the Brotherhood's staff because the union couldn't
pay them, and many others went without salaries, living
off savings or borrowing from friends so that they could
continue the fight for the union. The Brotherhood had
touched bottom.

Then, during this terrible time, a letter arrived in the mail. It was from a man who was known to have connections with the Pullman Company. Randolph opened it and found a check for $10,000. The note accompanying the check said: "You have done all anyone could be expected to do. Now that the cause is lost, please accept this check as a reward and take a trip to Europe."

Phil was furious. "Do they think they can buy me?" he said through clenched teeth. He turned the check over and over. A lesser man might have reasoned that the fight was lost, taken the money, and given up. But Randolph saw things differently. The porters had sacrificed everything. Some had been fired. Some had lost their pensions. Some went into debt. They went hungry and sometimes homeless for the cause of the Brotherhood. How could he betray them now? In the darkness of the hard days that were upon them, Randolph was still convinced that ultimately the Brotherhood would win. He was sure that black men would be able to form a strong union; he would not abandon the cause. He put the check back in the envelope and, with a hand trembling with rage at the insult to his integrity, sent it back.

The story spread among the porters that Randolph had sent back a check for $10,000. This was more money than any of the men could ever hope to see in their lives. They knew Randolph had no money of his own, that he could barely pay his own rent, and that he lost his beloved *Messenger* in the fight for the union. Here was a man to trust; here was a man who could not be bought! The idea of the Brotherhood took on a new life because of his unselfish act. Many porters felt that "if Mr. Randolph could give up such a gift, then I can at least rejoin the union."

Randolph told his story before meetings of porters.

I will not take Pullman gold. The Pullman Company thinks it can buy the Brotherhood, but they are wrong. They don't know the New Negro. They don't know of the newer spirit of the race which places beliefs above dollars. The Brotherhood is showing black men and women, and Pullman officials, that money is not everything, and that the spirit and the will of the people for justice is unconquerable.

There was a new spirit in the Brotherhood. The movement began to revive and although its prospects didn't seem any better, there was the widespread feeling that the Brotherhood would win, no matter how long it took. Randolph set out to rebuild the union. First, he needed allies. The failure of the strike threat proved that the Brotherhood was too weak to be without powerful friends. His aim was to get the AFL to recognize the Brotherhood as a member union.

Although he had been so critical of the AFL in the past, even calling it a stronghold of racism that should be broken up, he now needed its support. President William Green, he felt, was in sympathy with the porters. He had often spoken to Brotherhood meetings and had advised Randolph. Green seemed to be honest in his beliefs that black workers should be unionized, and even though he had done nothing to end the racism of member unions, Randolph felt he could be counted on to help.

But even getting into the AFL proved difficult. Other unions claimed jurisdiction, saying that since porters performed work that was similar to that done by their members, they alone had the right to organize the porters. One such union was the hotel alliance, which said that the porters weren't really railroad men, but were more like hotel employees. But Randolph said that the alliance had discriminated against black workers. "We will never allow the Brotherhood to become a small segregated part of your union," he declared. "Our men have sacrificed too much to give up their own union for second-class status in yours."

But as long as the hotel alliance insisted on its right to organize the porters, the Federation would not admit the Brotherhood as a full-fledged member union. So, in 1929, a compromise was reached. The AFL's leadership decided that the Brotherhood's thirteen local unions would each become "federal unions"—the all-black unions directly under the control of the AFL, rather than one of its member unions.

Randolph objected to this. There was no reason, he said, why the Brotherhood should not be admitted to the AFL on the same basis as any other national union, with its own central office and its own leadership. He used this situation to launch an attack on the whole practice of federal unions for blacks. Members of federal unions, he said, had to pay higher dues. Their votes were worth less at the AFL conventions too. Each federal union could cast but one vote, so the thirteen locals that made up the Brotherhood would have only thirteen votes. But if they were allowed to join the AFL as one union—the Brotherhood of Sleeping Car Porters—they would have forty votes, since each union's vote was based on the number of members it had.

Finally, federal unions were just a device to keep blacks out of some of the AFL's member unions. "Racial unions," Randolph charged, "have no justification for existing, any more than do unions based on religion, sex, or nationality." But once more, the AFL fell back on its old excuse—that it could not force member unions to accept blacks and that the federal unions were still a good way for blacks to be part of the labor movement. Randolph had to accept this for the moment. He knew he needed the Federation more than the Federation needed the porters. He swallowed his pride and decided to fight the battle against racism from within the ranks of the AFL. "You have not heard the last of this," he told President Green.

Another all-white union, the Order of Sleeping Car Conductors, tried to get jurisdiction over the porters. In 1934 the AFL's leaders decided to let the porters be taken over by the conductors' union. "We will not submit to this," Randolph exploded. "If necessary, we will withdraw from the AFL and become an independent union. Just try to explain to the black workers of this country how you dare to take the union we have built through such sacrifices and turn it over to another union that has a white-only clause in its constitution."

Finally, the AFL gave up. It saw that it could not break the spirit of Randolph or the porters. A group that withstood the worst the Pullman Company could do would resist discrimination by organized labor. In 1935 the AFL announced that it would admit the Brotherhood as a full member union, and the next summer William Green traveled to Chicago, the home of the Pullman Company, to present the charter to Phil Randolph at a mass meeting of the black community. The Brotherhood was now officially the equal of the 105 "international" unions of the AFL—the first black union to achieve this status.

Even before this final triumph within the Federation, the Brotherhood was regaining the confidence of the porters who had left it after the strike threat failed. The AFL's backing in those dark days helped. So did two grants from the Garland Fund, a foundation whose gifts enabled the Brotherhood to rebuild its shattered hopes. And Randolph was able to start a newspaper to replace the lost *Messenger*.

He called the union's newspaper *The Black Worker*. When people first heard of it, they were shocked. *Black* wasn't in favor in those days. In fact, the word was never used. Even *Negro* wasn't considered to have much status. And *Worker*! "Why not Railroad Man, or some other title?" Randolph was asked. "With a title like *Black Worker* you are associating yourself with lower-class life and rejecting higher-sounding names."

"That's why I'm calling it by that name," Randolph answered. "There is nothing to be ashamed of in being black and in being a worker. We must help build a consciousness of pride in race and in the working class." So, many years before "Black Is Beautiful" became widespread, Phil Randolph was building black pride and working-class pride.

Through the pages of *The Black Worker* and through hundreds of meetings all over the country, Randolph continued to spread the gospel of unionism and win allies for the porters' cause, but the road was all uphill, since the country was reeling from the effects of the worst economic depression in its history. Millions of people were out of work. Factories were closed and machines silent. Everyone felt the grip of fear. In 1932 a new President was elected—Franklin D. Roosevelt. He told the country that "the only thing we have to fear is fear itself," and his new administration busily started to get the country moving again. Roosevelt openly declared himself a friend of labor, and Randolph began to look for ways in which the new President could help the porters win their fight with Pullman.

If only porters were covered by the railroad laws, Randolph thought. And then the solution became obvious. "We will ask the President to have the railroad laws changed so that we too will be protected by them," he said.

Although Randolph had been severely criticized for supporting the AFL, his policy now paid off. He called on President Green and asked him, as the head of the most powerful labor organization in the country, to put pressure on the White House to change the law. Randolph went before Congress to explain how important it was for the porters to come under the railroad laws that protected workers and gave them the right to form unions. Thanks to his friendship with William Green, even the racist railroad unions testified in his favor.

In 1934 Congress added amendments to the Railway Labor Act. The porters now had the right to form a union and the Pullman Company would have to deal with them. It could no longer refuse to recognize a legitimate union.

Randolph immediately wrote the company to ask for a meeting. But Pullman was still taking its tough line. "There is no occasion for a conference with you," Pullman wrote back, saying that the Brotherhood did not represent the porters. Again Randolph went to the Mediation Board in Washington, which ordered an election. The porters would vote on whether they wished the Brotherhood to represent them. The result was another victory for the union. Almost six thousand porters voted for it, with only fourteen hundred votes for what was left of the old company union. The deep, dark days of post-strike 1928 were forgotten as the porters flocked to the union's banner. By 1935 the Brotherhood was no longer a semi-secret group of men defying a powerful company. Under the law, it was now the legal representative of all the porters, and the company would have to do what it always said it would never do—sit down with Phil Randolph and negotiate as equals.

The company would have to abide by the law, but it wasn't going to go down without a fight. Once again it tried to buy Randolph off. One day Randolph and his friend, porter official William Bowe, visited the home of a man they suspected was a company spy. There was a stranger there, a man from Chicago.

"Mr. Randolph," the stranger said, "the Pullman Company is willing to pay any reasonable sum to see you leave the Brotherhood. It is willing to negotiate, but it prefers not to deal with you." He pulled a check out of his pocket. It was dated and signed: only the amount was left blank. "Here," the stranger said, offering a pen, "all you have to do is write in the figure."

Randolph smiled. Before, when he had received a check for $10,000 in the mail, it looked like the company was doing him a favor, almost like sending flowers to his funeral. But this new offer was, to him, an admission that the company was beaten. The law, the government, and all of organized labor was now on the porters' side.

"I'm sorry to disappoint you," Randolph said, "but I'm not for sale. Tell your employers in Chicago that Phil Randolph can't be bought."

Negotiations between the union and the company dragged on for two years. The company used every trick it could think of to delay serious talks, hoping that the Brotherhood's support among its members would melt away when they saw that there was still no contract. It postponed meetings, pleading that its officials were ill, or had to be elsewhere on company business. It haggled endlessly over a word here or a comma there. And sometimes Pullman negotiators tried to bully the Brotherhood men. C. L. Dellums recalls one of these meetings in Chicago:

They had one of these big fellows, a vulgar character, who would come into the conference room only when we were talking about money. He would lay back and tap his foot against the table and curse like a drunken sailor. He made the Chief so angry. One day they were so angry they were pointing their fists and fingers at each other. I've never seen the Chief angry like that before. The table was between them and they were too far apart to get to one another. This fellow was cursing, but the Chief didn't use bad language—he had a hard time saying "hell" or "damn." Finally the Chief couldn't take it any longer and he looked around at me and said, "C. L., you want to say something?"

I can't tell you what I said, but I took over. I told this character that Mr. Randolph was a natural born gentleman. I got in there with him and we went to it. I think I knew as many curse words as he did, and after we finished the meeting broke up.

Finally, the company realized it was beaten. On August 25, 1937—exactly twelve years after the founding of the Brotherhood in a small Harlem meeting hall,

Pullman officials and union leaders, led by Phil Randolph, trooped into a conference room in the Pullman Building in Chicago to sign a contract.

The Brotherhood was recognized as the sole spokesman for the porters, and immediate wage increases of nearly one-third were ordered. That meant the porters would get nearly $2 million a year in extra wages. Their hours of work were cut by one-third, and the amount of traveling they had to do was cut from eleven thousand miles a month to seven thousand miles.

It had been a long, hard struggle. The news of the triumph spread among the black people of America, whose spirits soared as high as the rainbow after the storm. The great news was celebrated at family dinners, at community picnics, and at church meetings. It was a cause for joy; a cause for happiness.

A small band of black workers had won. The porters were the largest black union in the country, and the first ever admitted to the AFL as full members; the first ever to win a federally sponsored election; the first to force a large corporation to deal with them; the first to be able to prove to blacks everywhere that in union there was strength and power; the first to win a huge contract victory that gave black workers more money for fewer hours.

Back in the Brotherhood's New York office, Randolph pondered the meaning of his victory. His desk was covered with mail and many of the letters invited him to speak at the many community celebrations. He was happy, of course, that all the pain and suffering of the past twelve years had finally ended. Now the first step is over, he thought, the step of proving that black workers can be organized into a union and can win better wages and working conditions. But the next step must be for black workers to win equality within the labor movement.

And Phil Randolph prepared himself for yet another struggle.

CHAPTER SEVEN

Fighting from Within

WHEN the Great Depression came, it hit black people hardest. The stock market crashed in October 1929. In the months that followed, banks closed their doors, companies failed, and workers lost their jobs by the thousands. But for black people, the Depression started early. A year before Wall Street ever dreamed that hard times were in store, 300,000 black industrial workers were jobless. And on the farms it was worse, with many rural blacks fleeing starvation by pouring into the cities of the North. They sought work, but there was none.

As the black poet Langston Hughes wrote: "The Depression brought everybody down a peg or two, and the Negroes had but few pegs to fall."

By 1933 it was estimated that two-thirds of Harlem's labor force was out of work. In Philadelphia, more than half of all black workers were jobless, and even two out of every five white workers were unemployed. In Birmingham, the steel capital of the South, three out of four blacks were without jobs. Nationally, one of every four black workers was unemployed, compared with one of every seven white workers.

These were terrible times. The only cash ever seen by hundreds of thousands of people who used to get regular paychecks was now in the form of welfare grants. Things were very bad for whites, but blacks, who were the last hired and the first fired, had it worse.

Black workers were even being forced from menial occupations once reserved for them by whites who thought it beneath their dignity to do manual labor. An Urban League report stated:

. . . white men are driving trucks and express wagons in the South, repairing streets, doing the scavenger work, delivering ice on their backs where formerly Negroes delivered and white men collected for deliveries, serving as waiters and bellmen in hotels and doing other tasks which were once regarded only fit for Negroes. This same practice passes beyond menial occupations to the building trades where impressive losses are felt keenly. . . . The transformation goes on in the North as well, where elevator operators, doormen, house servants, and hotel men are more often white than colored.

Part of the reason black workers were hit so hard by the Depression was that they weren't protected by unions. One out of every ten white workers was a union member, but only one of fifty blacks belonged to a union. About thirty major national unions wouldn't allow blacks as members. Some, like the Brotherhood of Locomotive Firemen and Engineers, even signed contracts with employers stipulating that no blacks were to be hired. Although there were 13,000 black electricians, only 334 were allowed into the electricians' union. Of the

6,000 black plasterers, only 100 were union men. Not one of the 3,500 black plumbers held a union card.

It was easy to see why blacks were bitter about the labor movement's failure to stop the discrimination that was costing black people jobs and income. As a black newspaper commented sharply: "Unless the AFL is able to make its locals throughout the country open their doors to colored members in all crafts, it may be necessary for colored labor to organize and join in a country-wide fight on the unions."

Phil Randolph shared their anger, but he would not give up his dream of unionism as a way for blacks to improve their lot. He had fought the AFL; even shouted for its downfall. But now he knew that it was dangerous to tear down the unions—they must be opened up instead. Throughout the early years of the Depression he was struggling to win union recognition and a contract for the Pullman porters, but at the same time, he was trying to change the American labor movement from within.

He still believed what he had written as a young man —that black and white labor must unite if workers were to change the system that oppressed them. Once the porters were a part of the AFL, Randolph was able to carry the fight into the inner meetings of the labor movement, a position that could be far more effective than his former one of taking potshots at it in the pages of *The Messenger*.

Each year the Federation met in a grand convention of all member unions. It was at these conventions that resolutions were passed and positions on major issues taken. Randolph, as president of the Brotherhood of Sleeping Car Porters, was now a delegate to the AFL conventions—he was no longer an outsider, but was in a position to plead the cause of black workers from within.

He attended his first convention as an observer, a guest of President William Green. That was in 1926, shortly after starting the porters' union. He wasn't impressed. Debates were dull and major issues weren't really discussed. There seemed to be a lack of genuine democracy at the meeting. And worst of all, the problems of black workers were not even mentioned. This saddened Randolph because, as he later wrote, "American labor needs the refreshing, spiritual idealism of the black American worker. It cannot reach its full flowering without him."

Phil Randolph was determined that blacks would no longer be ignored at future AFL conventions, and with Randolph hammering away at trade-union discrimination in private and public meetings, those conventions would no longer be dull either. At a time when the Brotherhood was trying to get official AFL support and was fighting off the jurisdictional claims of other unions, it might have seemed smart not to attack the labor movement's racial policies. Another man might have tried to play ball with the Federation and not raise issues that would make enemies for the union. But Phil Randolph saw his role as speaking out for justice for all black workers and would not compromise.

He kept hammering away at union discrimination. In 1933 he demanded that the AFL hire black union organizers who would travel through the South to enlist black workers in unions "in large numbers." Labor, Randolph said, "has to remove from the hands of the employing class the weapon of race prejudice."

The following year he asked the AFL to throw out any

union that kept out black workers. Randolph charged that the color bar was "unsound, defenseless, undemocratic, illegal, and un-American." His proposal threw the assembled labor leaders into panic, and it was voted down on the old excuse that the Federation could not interfere with member unions' internal policies. But Randolph counter-attacked by asking that President Green appoint a special committee to investigate union discrimination. While the convention feared going that far, it did agree to an investigation of "the conditions of colored workers in this country."

The committee held its hearings in the summer of 1935. Randolph testified, presenting a stack of documentary evidence that proved discrimination was keeping black workers from joining unions, and he showed how the system of all-black "federal" locals was harming black workers. Other civil rights leaders and groups testified. The committee was deluged with evidence and testimony that showed organized labor was a force in keeping black workers down.

The committee's report was all that Randolph had hoped for. It recommended a threefold plan for ending union racism. It called for all unions that discriminated against blacks to change their rules to assure equality for all workers. It proposed that the AFL refuse membership to unions seeking to join the Federation who still practiced discrimination. And it urged an educational campaign "to get the white worker to see more completely the weakness of division and the necessity of unity between white and black workers."

The report was supposed to be presented to the 1935 convention, where it would be voted on. But the AFL's leaders saw the report as a package of dynamite that would split the labor movement. So President Green turned it over to George Harrison, president of the lily-white railway clerks' union, who rewrote it completely, dropping all the tough sections and leaving only a vague call for education.

The 1935 convention was a long, drawn-out affair marked by the struggle between craft and industrial unions that eventually led to a breakup of the Federation. Late in the last night of the convention, with the delegates tired of debate and anxious to go home, Harrison's report was tossed onto the pile of unfinished business. Randolph was furious at this betrayal. He charged that the report had been delayed "until such time when it will not be possible to have full discussion." Although it was late, he said, the issue was too important to cover up. Delegates groaned. Here was that troublemaker Randolph again. But Randolph didn't care what they thought of him; he would carry the fight for black workers to the convention floor no matter how late the hour.

The Harrison report, he charged, was "diplomatic camouflage" designed to bury the issue of discrimination. "The American Federation of Labor will not be able to hold its head up and face the world," he insisted, "so long as it permits any section of workers in America to be discriminated against because they happen to be black." Despite the lateness of the hour and the desire of the delegates to wind up the meeting, Randolph dug in for a full debate.

He delivered a long speech, the most complete analysis of black workers and the labor movement ever made at an AFL convention. At long last the issue that had always been hidden from public view was now out in the open.

He read the original report of the committee and showed
how Harrison had weakened it to the point where it was
meaningless. He explained all the different methods by
which unions discriminated against blacks. He showed
how the old argument that the Federation couldn't
change the practices of member unions was phony. The
AFL, he proved, had forced its affiliated unions to con-
form to national rules on many other issues in the past. It
was only on the issue of race that it suddenly decided it
couldn't force them to change.

Then he turned his guns on the black "federal" unions
and all-black locals that were attached to the all-white
national unions. He showed how these black locals
couldn't bargain for contracts themselves but had to allow the white national union to do it for them. He
proved how this and other traditional practices had
robbed the black worker of his bargaining power and of
union protection. There is no reason, Randolph said,
"why an organization of labor which is interested in the
organization of workers . . . should single out the
Negro workers and attach to them the stigma of in-
feriority."

The AFL's leaders paraded to the platform to defend
themselves. Harrison said that blacks in his union were
"separate but equal." Another union boss said that
Randolph's harsh words would "create prejudice." And
President Green said that, after all, only 5 AFL unions
out of 105 had color bars. Not true, Randolph answered:
20 unions openly keep blacks out and many more discriminate in other ways.

The debate dragged on into the night. Finally, it
ground to a halt. The convention voted to accept the
watered-down Harrison report. Randolph was beaten. At

the very moment when he was pressing the Federation and President Green to admit the Brotherhood as a full member union, he had touched off a bitter attack on the Federation itself and had challenged its president. It may have been bad politics, but to Philip Randolph, principles could not be compromised. It was something the Pullman Company was learning and now the labor movement would have to start to learn it too.

Shortly after the 1935 convention ended, the industrial unions formed their own organization, eventually leaving the AFL to form the Congress of Industrial Organizations (CIO). The CIO was based on the idea that all workers in an industry should belong to one union. The AFL held to the idea that each craft—such as plumbers, machinists, etc.—should belong to a separate union. Since the bulk of black workers were laborers or factory hands, and had no specialized craft, the CIO seemed to be a good way for blacks to become unionized. Randolph had always supported the idea of industrial unions and had joined hands with the AFL only because it was then the only national federation of labor unions.

The unions making up the new CIO had a more liberal attitude toward black workers. Some of its member unions, like the mine workers, had always admitted blacks as equals. And newer unions, like the auto workers, were outspoken in their support for blacks. For the first time, thousands of black workers in steel plants, packing houses, and rubber and textile plants found themselves members of powerful unions who sought to protect their rights on an equal basis with white members.

One of the most powerful of the CIO's leaders was John L. Lewis, the head of the mine workers. He was a friend of Randolph's and had supported him in his fight against AFL discrimination. One of Lewis's assistants had been on the committee that recommended strong measures against union racism and had resigned from the committee in protest when its report was weakened.

"Look, Phil," Lewis said. "Those guys over at the AFL haven't listened to you in all those years you were trying to get blacks accepted. Why don't you join us? Pull the Brotherhood out of the AFL and join the CIO. We want you."

"Why should I?" Randolph rejoined.

"Because we won't discriminate," Lewis said. "There will be no discrimination in the CIO."

Randolph smiled. "Are you sure, John?" he asked.

"I'm positive, Phil," Lewis shot back.

"Well then," Randolph replied. "That's why I have to stay in the AFL. That's where the action is."

And so Phil Randolph stayed where the action of the daily battle for the rights and dignity of black labor had to be fought. Year in and year out, AFL meetings and conventions would be marked by the distinguished-looking president of the Brotherhood slowly mounting the podium to deliver blistering attacks on the strongholds of labor racism. He never shouted, never ranted. Always, even when angered by slurs against black people, he kept his dignity and, armed with facts and figures, built his case for union democracy. Sometimes he was joined by other labor leaders, but often he stood alone in the long, weary fight.

In 1940 he tried once more to get a committee appointed to investigate discrimination against blacks. He proposed, since black workers were too poor to come to the AFL's offices in Washington, that a committee of both races travel around the country to gather information and make recommendations. True to form, the Federation voted against his plan. Randolph just shrugged his shoulders and plunged into further debate, attacking the discrimination of the big railroad unions and leading the fight for an independent union made up of the black redcaps and freight handlers.

In 1941 he pressed the attack against the federal unions once more, and tried to get the color bar removed from unions in the aircraft and shipbuilding industries. With the nation at the brink of war, these industries were hiring many new workers, but blacks were being shut out of them. Once again, he was met by the howls of indignation from the delegates. Speaker after speaker rose to defend union practices. All the old familiar arguments were trotted out. Discrimination existed before the AFL came into being and there was little it could do about it. Member unions controlled their own affairs. The federal union locals were perfectly all right. And so on into the night.

But Randolph took these arguments and chopped them up. He proved they were only a screen to mask racist discrimination that kept blacks out of good jobs.

The AFL was getting fed up with this persistent black man who turned every convention into a fight over the rights of black workers. The head of the carpenters' union asked why Randolph had to "merely criticize" the unions, and tell of "things that did not sound so well." If Randolph would tell of all the good things that were done for the Negro, he said, "he would do much more good for his race." Others were even more direct. The head of the teamsters shouted, "Sooner or later this kind of stuff will have to be stopped." And the head of the shipbuilders' union cried: "Some of us are getting a bit tired of being kicked around by professional agitators."

Through it all, Randolph pressed his attacks. Throughout the war years he continued to propose resolution after resolution calling for AFL action. The conventions voted them all down, even a plan to allow black soldiers to join member unions when they returned home from the war. But Randolph never got discouraged; never gave up his fight.

He became known as "the conscience of the AFL," and even those who opposed him respected his courage. William Green always lined up against Randolph's resolutions, but he admitted publicly that Randolph was "moved by a deep sense of injustice." It took the Pullman Company twelve years before it would sign a contract with the Brotherhood, and it would take longer for the AFL to change its attitudes about black workers. But Randolph felt that time was on his side and, as he chipped away at the phony excuses of the labor movement, he knew that each of his attacks would help to wear away its structure of racism.

"I have to be where the action is," Randolph had said. And the inner councils of the Federation became his battleground. Eventually he would become an honored officer of the Federation, and would see his proposals become accepted. But during the dark night of the thirties and forties, he was a lone battler in the wilderness of trade-union discrimination.

CHAPTER EIGHT

The National Negro Congress

DURING the 1930's Phil Randolph was active on three
fronts. He was head of the porters' union, locked in
combat with the Pullman Company, and fighting trade-
union discrimination within the AFL. And, in the
closing years of that decade, he stepped onto the national
stage as a powerful leader and spokesman for all black
people.

Randolph supported the growing boycott movements
among blacks, and his organizational skills and the man-
power of the porters' union helped blacks to win jobs
through non-violent direct action. The boycott movements started in the early thirties, as black people found
themselves jobless while forced to buy in neighborhood
stores that hired whites only. In Harlem, all of the stores
along 125th Street, the main shopping street, had white-
only employment policies. In Washington, a restaurant
in the heart of the black ghetto dismissed its black
workers and hired whites to replace them. In Chicago,

stores rejected black college graduates for sales jobs, hiring uneducated white people.

"Buy Black" campaigns were the answer to this discrimination. Black people were urged to buy only in those stores that hired black workers. Picket lines were thrown up around stores that refused to do so. These campaigns were truly grass roots affairs; that is, they were planned, staffed, and organized by local black citizens without much help from the national civil rights groups. Randolph was active in the campaign to open up jobs in Harlem, while Brotherhood men helped lead the fight in their own home towns.

But these campaigns could not really do much to lift the heavy burden of unemployment from the backs of black people. While many jobs were opened up for black workers, the Depression was too deep, and masses of black people remained hungry and jobless. In 1935 their anger and resentment overflowed, and Harlem was plunged into its first riot. A false rumor that a black boy had been beaten by a store owner touched off street rioting that led to the looting and smashing of hundreds of stores in Harlem and caused over $2 million worth of property damage.

New York's mayor, Fiorello La Guardia, appointed an investigating committee to search out the causes of the riot. He appointed Phil Randolph and eleven other prominent citizens, black and white. The committee became a People's Court, holding hearings in a small city courtroom in Harlem. Daily, black people trooped in to tell Randolph and the other investigators of their encounters with racism. Police brutality, job discrimination, cheating by store owners, and other abuses were recounted in the slow drawls of southern migrants and the quick patter of native black New Yorkers. No jobs, they all said. "The telephone company won't hire blacks," they cried. "The electric company says they only give jobs to whites," came the dismal story.

Finally, the committee filed its report. Like the reports of groups who investigated the 1919 Chicago riot and like the reports of investigators into the riots of the 1960's, the committee found that the cause of the social unrest was the lack of economic security for black people. Discrimination in employment loomed as the major cause of the riot.

The program of social reforms sponsored by President Roosevelt's administration, dubbed the New Deal, was putting some black people to work on federal projects, but not enough. As long as the country was in the midst of a Depression, black people would suffer, and it seemed as if very little could be done.

In 1935 a conference was held at Howard University in Washington, D.C., to study the problems affecting black people. It was at this conference that the idea of one national black agency that could mobilize all blacks to economic and political action was formulated. Under the leadership of Dr. Ralph Bunche (who won the Nobel Peace Prize in 1950 for his work with the United Nations) and John P. Davis, a meeting was called to form a National Negro Congress.

Randolph was enthusiastic about the idea. He wrote a special article for a booklet that outlined the objectives of the Congress.

On every fundamental problem a ringing and militant declaration of policy could be promulgated by such a Congress and since it would represent the collective expression and will

of millions of Negroes embraced in their various organizations, [neither] government nor industry could view it with
indifference and unconcern. . . . As more and more groups
come to understand the vital need of joint action and the
tremendous value of working together, as they come through
such joint action to a clearer and more friendly understanding of each other, we may expect to see the National Negro
Congress become increasingly useful in the struggles of the
Negro people in America.

The meeting, which Randolph helped to plan, was
held in Chicago in February 1936. More than 800 people
attended, representing 585 black civic clubs, church
groups, unions, and other organizations having a total
membership of over one million.

Randolph, in his keynote address, reflected the despair
black people felt during those grim days of the Depression. The government, he said, was more concerned with
saving the capitalistic system than with saving poor
people and black people from the ravages of hunger.
"The New Deal is no remedy," he declared. "It does not
seek to change the profit system. It does not place human
rights above property rights, but gives the business interests the support of the state."

The National Negro Congress backed a series of proposals to fight discrimination and to encourage black
unionism. A permanent organization was established
with local councils in several cities. And the meeting
elected Phil Randolph to be president of the NNC. John
P. Davis, who was elected executive secretary, would be
the man who ran the organization on a daily basis.

The next meeting was held in Philadelphia in 1937.
More than 1,100 people attended to hear a long list of

speakers, including the head of the NAACP, Walter White, and the president of the CIO, Philip Murray. The Congress passed 174 resolutions calling for reforms, and launched plans for increased local activity across the nation. With the full cooperation of the NAACP, the Urban League, and the CIO, it began to look like the National Negro Congress would become a powerful voice for the interests of black people.

But there were some rumblings of discontent that soon broke into the open. The presence of Communists among the NNC's members and leadership made many people fear that the group would be used for the benefit of the Communist party, and not for the benefit of black people. Professor Kelly Miller, a former associate of Booker T. Washington, wrote after the first convention:

"The spirit of radicalism predominated throughout the proceedings. The reds, the Socialists and Communists, were everywhere in ascendancy, either in number or indomitable purpose, or in both. The conservative delegates, who constituted a considerable proportion of the conference, were either outnumbered or out-maneuvered."

Randolph had not trusted the Communists. From the very beginning of the party, in the early 1920's, he warned that they were just following a line dictated by Moscow. The Socialism he believed in had no place for dictatorship or for anything that was not democratic. He prevented the Communists from having any influence in the Brotherhood. For that, as well as for his cooperation with the AFL, the Communists had bitterly attacked him as a reactionary stooge of racists. When the Communist party proposed that the answer to the Negro problem in America was the creation of an all-black state in the

South, he attacked the idea. Nearly all black people rejected the Communists' plan, and very few were attracted to the party.

But by the mid-thirties the Communist party had changed its line. It no longer called for a separate black state. Instead, it preached cooperation between Communists and non-Communists to achieve broad social reforms. This new policy, called the Popular Front, was formulated because the party believed that the twin threats of European Fascism under Hitler and the Great Depression could only be met through cooperative action. So the party's black vice-presidential candidate, James W. Ford, became one of the organizers of the NNC and party members joined it. Their real plan, which was not to be discovered until later, was to dominate the organization and control it for their own purposes.

While Randolph did not trust the Communists, he too felt that at a time of great crisis all groups, no matter what their philosophy, should band together "in a united front against Fascism and repression of the rights of Negroes." He was willing, as were so many other non-Communists, to bury his differences with them in pursuit of more important goals.

But in 1939 the Communist party changed its line once more. Russia had signed an agreement with Hitler's Germany. Where the Communists had once portrayed Hitler as the archenemy, they now did a complete flip-flop and said that Hitler and Stalin were the only peace-lovers around. The war against Germany that broke out in September 1939 was, they said, an imperialist war that should be rejected by workers all over the world.

Phil Randolph, like everyone else who had a grain of sense, knew this was ridiculous. Hitler was one of the

most bloodthirsty dictators in history, and just because
Communist Russia, for its own purposes, decided to
make a deal with him, that was no reason for sensible
people to abandon their democratic principles. As far as
Randolph was concerned, he wouldn't dance to the Communists' tune. He would continue to be against Hitler
and he felt the NNC should continue to fight militantly
for the black man's rights. The Communists, on the other
hand, wanted to use the NNC to attack President Roosevelt's foreign policy of helping England, France, and the
other victims of Hitler's mad ambitions.

The Popular Front was dead. From now on, the party
would launch an all-out attack on defense programs and
foreign aid and try to convince black people to set aside
their concerns about inequality at home. "It is fundamentally necessary," wrote a top Communist official, "to
extend the greatest assistance to the building of the National Negro Congress as the broad expression of anti-war
and anti-imperialist struggle."

The showdown came at the 1940 convention in Washington. Of the 1,200 delegates to the convention, only
800 were black, and many of them represented Commu-
nist-dominated unions and political groups. And so did
the white representatives, most of whom were sent by the
party in an attempt to stack the meeting. The Communists soon had the convention under their firm control.
They dominated the committees, passed the resolutions,
and hooted down their opponents. It became clear to
Randolph that the NNC was now just another arm of the
Communist party and he decided not to run for re-elec-
tion as president. In fact, he would leave the NNC alto-
gether, for he had no desire to be a member of an
organization that was using black people for its own ends.

Finally, it was his turn to speak. He was determined to tell the truth and to stand by his principles. He condemned the Communists for trying to wreck the organization, and pointed out that the American Communist party was getting its orders from Moscow. Warning that the NNC must stick to an action program on behalf of black people and that it must not follow orders from Moscow, Randolph said: "American Negroes will not long follow any organization which accepts dictation and control from any white organization."

But his voice was drowned out by the shouts and boos of the crowd. The Communists had once again marked Randolph as their archenemy and they planned a demonstration to keep him from speaking. The Communists and their allies walked out of the hall during Randolph's speech, shouting and yelling as they went. But he stood there, straight and tall, and continued until he was finished. When he walked off the platform, only a third of the audience was left. The Communists had done their job thoroughly.

Later, he announced the reasons why he was leaving the National Negro Congress.

The Congress should be uncontrolled and responsible to no one but the Negro people. . . . When the National Negro Congress loses its independence it loses its soul and has no further reason for being. It also forfeits and betrays the faith of the Negro masses.

The Congress is not truly a Negro Congress. Out of some 1,200 or more delegates, over 300 were white, which made the Congress look like a joke. It is unthinkable that the Jewish Congress would have Gentiles in it, or that a Catholic Congress would have Protestants in it, or that the famous All India Congress would have in it as members natives of Africa. Why should a Negro Congress have white people in it?

The breakup of the Congress could not have come at a worse time. War was raging in Europe and the Depression for white workers was ending as factories that had gathered dust during the lean years of the thirties were now producing the ships, planes, tanks, and armaments of war. Work was becoming plentiful again, but for whites only. The Depression was still on full blast for blacks.

More than ever, black people needed an organization that would take the lead in winning their full political and economic rights. Now the NNC was just another Communist front group as almost all of its non-Communist members followed Randolph out of the organization. It was time to continue the fight for justice in other ways.

CHAPTER NINE

The March on Washington Movement

"WHILE we are in complete sympathy with the Negro, it is against company policy to employ them as aircraft workers or mechanics . . . regardless of their training, but there will be some jobs as janitors for Negroes." So spoke the president of North American Aviation, one of the biggest aircraft builders in America, in 1941.

He was not alone. A steel company head told the Urban League: "We haven't had a Negro worker in twenty-five years and do not plan to start now."

In the booming defense-industry plants, white men stood at machines and the handful of black employees pushed brooms. The nation was ferverishly preparing for its eventual entry into the war, but employers and unions prevented blacks from getting the high-paying jobs that were now available. Militant blacks threw up picket lines in front of factories, with signs that read:

HITLER MUST OWN THIS PLANT,
NEGROES CAN'T WORK HERE

IF WE MUST FIGHT, WHY CAN'T WE WORK?

When blacks picketed the Boeing Aircraft plant in Seattle, demanding jobs, the machinists' union district chief wailed: "Labor has been asked to make many sacrifices in this war and has made them gladly, but this sacrifice is too great." The Tampa Shipbuilding Corporation had six hundred black workers. Then it signed a union contract agreeing to hire only union members, but since the union refused membership to the blacks, within a year the six hundred jobs had dwindled to a handful of janitors' positions.

Just as the defense industry was mobilizing for war under the Jim Crow banner, so too were the armed forces. In September 1940 the draft went into effect. Young men would be forced to serve in the armed forces, but the old policy of separate units for black soldiers was unchanged. As in World War I, blacks would be kept in labor battalions while whites would get the chance to fight.

Black leaders were furious. How can this country fight for what it calls democracy, they asked, if blacks are kept second-class citizens? Just two weeks after President Roosevelt signed the new draft law, he met with a delegation of black leaders who came to Washington to protest discrimination in the armed forces. Phil Randolph was there, along with Walter White of the NAACP and T. Arnold Hill of the Urban League.

The black leaders argued for complete integration of the armed forces and an end to discrimination in defense factories. They left the White House in a hopeful mood, for the President promised to look into the ways in which discrimination could be lessened, and he said that blacks would serve in all branches of the army. But a few weeks later, the government declared that: "The policy of the War Department is not to intermingle colored and white enlisted personnel in the same regimental organizations."

In other words, blacks would once more be forced into inferior roles in a Jim Crow army. An outcry of protest by Randolph and the other black leaders, who charged that this policy was "a stab in the back of democracy," had little effect. Colonel Benjamin O. Davis was appointed the first black general in the country's history, and the army promised to train a black air force unit, but that's as far as Washington was willing to go.

Once again, black people would be condemned to joblessness, shifted into all-black army units, and victimized by racism. During the First World War, this took place under the slogan of "making America safe for democracy." Now it was to happen again, under similarly empty slogans. Randolph and others again asked to see the President, but Roosevelt was in no mood to sit through another session with them. He kept putting off another meeting until it became clear that he had no intention of seeing them.

Not even mass protests seemed to sway the government. Five thousand blacks demonstrated for defense jobs in Kansas City in December. The NAACP held protest meetings in twenty-six states in January 1941. Still no sign of change from the White House. As Walter White wrote: "Discontent and bitterness were growing like wildfire among Negroes all over the country."

Something more was needed; something on a scale never before seen; something that would dramatize the black man's plight to the world and at the same time unify America's 15 million black people. "Black people will not get justice," Randolph said, "until the administration leaders in Washington see masses of Negroes— ten, twenty, fifty thousand—on the White House lawn."

Randolph called White to tell him of his plan for a mass march on Washington by ten thousand or more black people. "If we can show the President that thousands of people are angry about this discrimination; if we can show him that they're upset enough to leave their homes and come all the way to the capital to protest, why, then he might do something."

White agreed. Others were brought in—Lester Granger, the head of the Urban League; Frank Crosswaith, Randolph's old comrade-in-arms and a fellow Socialist labor organizer; teachers; lawyers; churchmen. They all rallied behind this bold plan. Today we are used to mass demonstrations in Washington. Years before, in 1894, unemployed whites had done it. In 1932 war veterans had camped in Washington demanding bonus payments. But in 1941 it was unheard of for so many black people to assemble in the still-segregated capital. Even some blacks were doubtful that it could be done. "Where are you going to get ten thousand Negroes to march?" they asked. But Randolph was confident.

"Everything else has failed," Randolph said. "Only power can affect the enforcement and adoption of a given policy, and power is the active principle of only the organized masses, the masses united for a definite purpose." Black people would march, he said, and they would march under the slogan: "We loyal Negro American citizens demand the right to work and fight for our country."

The administration ignored the talk of a march. No one really expected black people to be able to do it. Then Randolph issued his "Call to Negro America to March on Washington for Jobs and Equal Participation in National Defense on July 1, 1941." Randolph's call to action was eloquent in its appeal to black people to stand up for their rights, and it was bold and forceful in its demand for equality:

Dear fellow Negro Americans, be not dismayed in these terrible times. You possess power, great power. Our problem is to hitch it up for action on the broadest, daring, and most gigantic scale.

In this period of power politics, nothing counts but pressure, more pressure, and still more pressure, through the tactic and strategy of broad, organized, aggressive mass action behind the vital and important issues of the Negro. To this end we propose that ten thousand Negroes MARCH ON WASHINGTON FOR JOBS IN NATIONAL DEFENSE AND EQUAL INTEGRATION IN THE FIGHTING FORCES OF THE UNITED STATES.

An "all-out" thundering march on Washington, ending in a monster and huge demonstration at Lincoln's Monument will shake up white America.

It will shake up official Washington. . . .

It will gain respect for the Negro people.

It will create a new sense of self-respect among Negroes.

And he made the march's goals very clear:

The Negroes' stake in national defense is big. It consists of jobs, thousands of jobs. It may represent millions, yes, hundreds of millions of dollars in wages. It consists of new industrial opportunities and hope. This is worth fighting for.

Most important and vital to all, Negroes, by the mobilization and coordination of their mass power, can cause PRESIDENT ROOSEVELT TO ISSUE AN EXECUTIVE ORDER ABOLISHING DISCRIMINATION IN ALL GOVERNMENT DEPARTMENTS, ARMY, NAVY, AIR CORPS, AND NATIONAL DEFENSE JOBS.

Early in June, with less than a month to go before the march took place, there were signs that the administration was worried. Black churches and community organizations were beginning to charter buses, and black ghettos all over the country were stirring. Randolph pulled together many of the largest black organizations into a March on Washington committee that was laying the groundwork for the big event. Government officials finally began to believe that there might be a march after all, and worried that it would be a blow to the nation's prestige, especially since the United States was painting itself as the arsenal of democracy.

The President's wife was a strong fighter for civil rights, and she knew many of the top black leaders. In fact, she often helped them by persuading the President to take steps to aid black people. On June 10, Eleanor Roosevelt wrote Randolph that she discussed the March with the President, and expressed her fears that Randolph was "making a very grave mistake. . . . I am afraid it will set back the progress which is being made," she wrote.

A few days later she came to New York to meet Randolph, Walter White, and others in Mayor La Guardia's office. "You know where I stand," she said. "But the attitudes of the Washington police, most of them Southerners, and the general feeling of Washington itself are such that I fear that there may be trouble if the March occurs."

She and the Mayor both promised that the President would do something to stop job discrimination. But the March should be called off so that the government would have time to act. But Randolph said: "Mrs. Roosevelt, we are busily engaged in mobilizing our forces all over the nation for the March, and could not think of calling it off unless we have accomplished our definite aim, which is jobs, not promises."

"But such a march is impractical. You say you will be able to get twenty-five thousand or more Negroes to come to Washington. Where will they stay, where will they eat?" Mrs. Roosevelt asked worriedly.

"Why," said Randolph, "they'll stay in the hotels and eat in the restaurants." Washington was a southern city. Black people were not allowed into the hotels and restaurants outside the ghetto. When she heard Randolph's answer, Mrs. Roosevelt understood that what faced the government was not merely an embarrassing demonstration, but the threat of terrible violence, for white people would not casually allow this.

Then Randolph turned to Mayor La Guardia, an old friend of his who had once, during the darkest days of the Pullman battle, offered him a good job at City Hall. "Fiorello," Randolph smiled, "I should tell you that we will also march on City Hall."

"Why?" asked La Guardia. "What have I done?"

"We will march," Randolph said, "to publicly ask you to ask the President to issue an executive order to end this shameful discrimination."

The next day Randolph got a phone call from a government official. "The President would like you to come to the White House to discuss your March," the caller said. A few days later Roosevelt publicly condemned job discrimination and ordered his defense production chiefs to do something about it.

Perhaps Roosevelt thought this would satisfy the March committee. It didn't. Randolph immediately said the President's statement was ineffective, and he promised that the March would be "the greatest demonstration of Negro mass power for our economic liberation ever conceived." It would be the "technique and method of action that is the hope and salvation of the Negro people."

On June 18 Randolph and White met with Roosevelt. The President told them he was opposed to the March. He said that the navy and the army would not integrate their forces, but that he'd be willing to set up a special committee to investigate complaints of discrimination in employment.

"Mr. President," Randolph said, "we need jobs right now, not tomorrow or the day after, but now."

Roosevelt said he understood such strong feelings, but insisted that a march was not the way to win progress. "What if other minorities were to march on Washington?" he asked. "It would create resentment among the American people because such a march would be considered as an effort to coerce the government and make it do certain things."

Randolph answered that there was no comparison between the relatively mild discrimination other minorities were experiencing and the terrible situation black people faced. The March, he said, was a reasonable method of

bringing grievances before the public. Roosevelt dis-
agreed. "The idea of a march is bad and unintelligent,"
he said, "and it will do more harm than good."

The President then turned to Walter White, head of
the NAACP, which was the largest organization con-
nected with the March. He could tell whether 10,000,
25,000, or 50,000 black people would come to Washington. "Walter, how many people will *really* march?"

"No less than 100,000, Mr. President," White replied.

Roosevelt looked deep into White's blue eyes as if
searching for the real truth. White, a courageous Negro
leader, was light-skinned and had often passed for white
while investigating lynchings in the South for the
NAACP. Once, in a Deep South town, a man laughingly
greeted him in the street, saying, "You gonna be around
for the fun tonight? There's a yalla nigger in town passin'
for white and we're gonna lynch him." White used his
common sense and caught the next train out of town.

Now he stared the President down. He himself wasn't
sure the March would be a success, but he didn't want
Roosevelt to know it. The President slowly turned his
gaze away. *A hundred thousand!* Visions of a race riot
formed in his mind. "What do you want me to do?" he
asked.

"We want you to issue an executive order abolishing
discrimination in war industries and in the armed
forces," Randolph answered.

The President appointed some government officials to
prepare a draft of an executive order that would satisfy
the black leaders. They left the White House with victory within their grasp. Teams of government lawyers
stayed up late drafting and re-drafting the order. "Ran-

dolph won't take this" and "Randolph wants that" filled
the air. Finally one young lawyer shouted, "Who the hell
is this Randolph, anyway?"

There seemed to be no way to compromise with the
iron-willed black man who was on a crusade for jobs for
his people. Just a week before the March, on June 24, La
Guardia met with Randolph. The President, he said, was
going to issue an executive order banning discrimination
in defense industries. "Well, Phil, you've got what you
want," the peppery Mayor said.

Randolph looked over the draft of the order. "I'm
sorry, but this won't do," Randolph said. "This does
nothing to stop government agencies from discrimination
in employment." Once more, the text was changed to
satisfy Randolph.

On June 25, 1941, President Roosevelt issued Executive Order 8802 declaring "that there shall be no discrimination in the employment of workers in defense
industries or government because of race, creed, color, or
national origin." The document ordered all government
agencies involved in defense production to "take special
measures . . . to assure that such programs are adminis-
tered without discrimination." It ordered that all government contracts with defense industries include anti-
discrimination promises.

Finally, it set up a Fair Employment Practices Committee. This committee, which became known as FEPC,
was to hold hearings to investigate complaints of discrimination and to take steps to end them either by
negotiation or by recommending action by the President
or government agencies.

A few days later, Randolph went on nationwide radio

to announce that the July 1 March on Washington would
be called off. Black people had won a great victory, he
declared, but they must continue to fight for justice. The
July 1 March would not take place—that was the price of
the executive order. But if the government didn't back
up its order, the March would take place on another date.
And Randolph said he was not disbanding the nationwide network of black organizations that he had mobi-
lized to pressure the government.

"It is my aim," Randolph told the nation, "to broaden
and strengthen the Negro March on Washington committees all over the United States, to serve as watchdogs
on the application of the President's executive order to
determine how industries are complying with it."

The howls of fury from the South and from some
employers and labor leaders that greeted the order were
drowned in the shouts of joy welling up from the black
community. The March's leaders didn't get everything
they asked for—the armed forces were still Jim Crowed
—but what they did win was the most important break-
through for black people since Reconstruction times.
Some black newspapers called it the most important
presidential order since the Emancipation Proclamation.
It marked the start of the federal government's active
role in civil rights, a role that was to grow much greater
in the years ahead.

The March idea demonstrated that if black people
would cooperate and organize to fight for specific goals,
they could win important victories. The goals and tactics
Randolph devised for the March would become the same
ones used later, in the great civil rights struggles of the
1960's.

Honors showered in on Randolph for his leadership of the March organization. He was called the "author of FEPC," won the most important award in the black community, the NAACP's Spingarn Medal, received an honorary degree from Howard University, and was named to the Schomburg Collection Honor Roll.

But the greatest honor Randolph won from his fight for jobs for blacks was the knowledge that he had led a revolution in the black man's economic status. A large part of the big gains blacks won during the war was due to the executive order Randolph forced the President to issue. By the end of the war, in 1945, there were about 1.25 million black union members, over six times more than there were in 1940. Black skilled craftsmen doubled between 1940 and 1944. Blacks in federal government jobs also doubled in that period. Black men's wages rose sharply—in 1940 the typical black family earned only about 40 percent of what the typical white family earned. By war's end, it was almost 60 percent as much.

Black workers were trading in their brooms for positions on the assembly lines and workbenches, and were helping to turn out the ships, planes, and arms that would defeat Hitler. Employers who once wouldn't hire a black man now set up training and hiring programs. And a year after the President's executive order was issued, the president of North American Aviation, who had earlier said that he wouldn't hire blacks, now declared: "Our Negro workmen have turned out swell. The spirit of these men is just as good as you'll find. They work hard and they know we are at war."

Phil Randolph's war was just begun. At fifty-two, he was at the height of his career.

As the *Amsterdam News,* a black weekly, put it:

"A. Philip Randolph, courageous champion of the rights of his people, takes the helm as the nation's No. 1 Negro leader. . . . already he is being ranked with the great Frederick Douglass."

Leaders of the Brotherhood of Sleeping Car Porters at Harlem's Elks Hall. A. Philip Randolph is fifth from the left and Ashley Totten is sixth from the left.

UPI

Mrs. Eleanor Roosevelt joined Randolph at a New York rally to save the Fair Employment Practices Committee in 1946.

In 1948, Randolph and Grant Reynolds (at left) told the Senate Armed Services Committee that blacks would refuse to register for the draft or serve in the military if racial segregation and discrimination were not ended.

Wide World Photos

At the Democratic National Convention in 1948, Randolph (far
left) led a demonstration outside Philadelphia's Convention
Hall to protest Jim Crow military service.

The March on Washington for Jobs and Freedom, August 28,
1963. Randolph is at the far right of the front line, and Martin
Luther King, Jr., near the center.

The March leaders met with the President. From left to right: Martin Luther King, Jr.; Rabbi Joachim Prinz, chairman of the American Jewish Congress; Randolph; President John F. Kennedy; and Walter Reuther, vice-president of the AFL-CIO.

In 1964, President Lyndon B. Johnson presented Randolph with
the Presidential Medal of Freedom.

Civil rights leaders at the NAACP headquarters in New York in 1964. From left to right: Bayard Rustin, Washington March leader; Jack Greenberg, NAACP lawyer; Whitney M. Young, Jr., National Urban League executive director; James Farmer, national CORE director; Roy Wilkins, executive secretary of the NAACP; Martin Luther King, Jr., president of the Southern Christian Leadership Conference; John Lewis, chairman of the Student Non-violent Coordinating Committee; A. Philip Randolph; and Courtney Young, of the student group.

A. Philip Randolph's eightieth birthday dinner, held at the Waldorf Astoria in New York in 1969. Left to right: Bayard Rustin, George Meany, Coretta King, Randolph, and Governor Nelson Rockefeller.

Sam Reiss

A. Philip Randolph

CHAPTER TEN

War on Two Fronts

EARLY on the morning of December 7, 1941, the Pacific sky was blanketed by wave after wave of Japanese bombers, flying out of the rising sun to attack the U.S. naval base at Pearl Harbor. When they completed their mission and wheeled back toward their home fields, the ships of the American Pacific fleet lay at the bottom of the ocean or in twisted masses of steel rubble at their docks. The United States was at war.

Phil Randolph had fought the country's entry into World War I. But this war was different—Japan's aggressive militarism and Nazi Germany's rabid racism had to be defeated: Just as he supported American aid to the Allies in the period before the United States' entry into the fighting, he now backed the country's struggle for total victory.

But he would not sacrifice his principles. Black people, he said, must help the country win the war, but they must also continue their fight against racism at home and help make the war into a social revolution, as well. "This is not a war for freedom," he wrote. "It is not a war for democracy. . . . It is a war between the imperialism of Fascism and Nazism and the imperialism of monopoly capitalistic democracy. Under neither are the colored peoples free. But this war need not be a world movement of reaction. The people can make it a People's Revolution."

Randolph believed that the war could become a struggle of the people of the world to free themselves from colonialism and injustice. He wanted China and India free from domination by other countries, and an Africa that was no longer ruled by European powers. At home, he wanted equality for black people. One of the great issues of the war, he declared, is: "Shall we have democracy for all of the people or for some of the people?" He saw the fight for black freedom in the United States as part of the world war against Nazi racism.

Randolph believed that black people had to be organized to wage their war for freedom, and so he decided to continue his March on Washington movement. The President's executive order had banned discrimination in defense industries, but that order now had to be enforced. And the armed forces were still segregated. A March on Washington committee, backed up by the threat to bring many thousands of black citizens in a mass protest march on the capital, was Randolph's vehicle to keep up the pressure on the government. "The Negro must fight for his democratic rights now," he insisted, "for after the war it may be too late."

His new movement demanded an end to Jim Crow laws in the South, new laws to give black people their constitutional rights, an end to lynching and to the poll tax that kept blacks from voting, an end to segregation in the armed forces, and an end to discrimination in jobs and in government. Every one of Randolph's demands eventually were brought about, but it would take more than two decades of constant pressure and black militancy to do it.

Randolph insisted that the March on Washington committee be all black; no white people could be members. He was severely criticized for this. Some people said this was reverse racism, and others charged that Randolph had adopted the black nationalism of the Garvey movement he fought in the twenties.

But Randolph had two very good reasons for keeping his movement all black. First, he believed that black people needed to prove that they could organize themselves into effective action. "The Negro," Randolph said, "must supply the money and pay the price, make the sacrifices and endure the suffering to break down his barriers." And he wanted "the President and the country not to be left in any doubt that this March was the symbol and expression of discontent and resentment of Negroes themselves against discrimination."

Such a mass effort could also unite the black community because it was a "form of struggle for Negro rights in which all Negroes can participate, including the educated and the so-called uneducated, the rich and the poor. It is a technique and strategy in which the 'little Negro' in the tavern, poolroom, on the streets; jitterbug, storefront preacher, and sharecropper can use to help free the race."

A second reason for keeping the movement all black

was to keep the Communists out. Randolph didn't want to give them a chance to take over the March the way they had the National Negro Congress. "They have their feet in America but their heads and hearts in Moscow," he charged. Now that Hitler was at war with Russia, the Communist line changed once more; they were now against militant demands for black equality on the grounds that it would hamper the war effort, which was of paramount importance. Where the *Daily Worker,* the Communist party's newspaper, had written in 1941: "You can't defend Negro rights without fighting the war," it now wrote: "The Negro people cannot be true to their own best interests without supporting the war."

But Randolph, who spent his whole life striving for interracial cooperation, was disturbed by charges that he was becoming racist. There is nothing wrong, he said, with black people organizing themselves, and there's nothing racist about it.

The March on Washington movement is an all-Negro movement, but it is not anti-white, anti-American, anti-labor, anti-Catholic, or anti-Semitic. It's simply pro-Negro. It does not rest so much upon race as upon the social problem of Jim Crow. It does not oppose interracial organizations. It cooperates with such mixed organizations as the National Association for the Advancement of Colored People and the National Urban League, and churches, trade unions. Its validity lies in the fact that no one will fight as hard to remove and relieve pain as he who suffers from it. Negroes are the only people who must take the initiative and assume the responsibility to abolish it. Jews must and do lead the fight against anti-Semitism, Catholics must lead the fight against anti-Catholicism, labor must battle against anti-labor laws and practices.

Randolph planned many actions for his March movement, but he always stressed non-violence. He was a follower of the Indian nationalist leader, Mahatma Gandhi, who preached a philosophy of non-violent resistance to evil. Many years later, this would become the main technique of the civil rights movement under Dr. Martin Luther King, Jr., and blacks and whites would violate the South's Jim Crow laws and not resist or take violent action when they were attacked. Just as Gandhi's non-violent movement eventually drove the British out of India, King's movement helped end overt racial segregation. But few people remember that it was A. Philip Randolph who first built a black mass movement founded on non-violent civil disobedience.

The March on Washington movement's rallies and demonstrations were typical of what Randolph called "non-violent, goodwill, direct action." At one point, he planned a one-week program of civil disobedience, in which black people would refuse to obey Jim Crow laws—not send their children to the segregated school, refuse to ride the segregated bus, sit at a whites-only lunch counter.

"Mass social pressure in the form of marches and picketing will not only touch and arrest the attention of the powerful public officials, but also the 'little man' in the street," he declared. "Before this problem of Jim Crow can be successfully attacked, all of America must be shocked and awakened."

To keep up the pressure, Randolph staged a series of giant rallies in several cities in 1942. The biggest took place in New York, where Harlem was plastered with leaflets demanding:

WAKE UP, NEGRO AMERICA!
Do you want work? Do you want equal
rights? Do you want Justice?
Then prepare now to fight for it!
50,000 NEGROES MUST STORM
MADISON SQUARE GARDEN
MOBILIZE NOW!

And the rally would be accompanied by a mass demonstration of support by those who could not attend.
"BLACK OUT HARLEM JUNE 16TH" shouted the
headline on the Brotherhood's magazine, *The Black
Worker*. Randolph's plan was simple. On the night of the
rally, stores would be closed and all electric lights shut off
in stores and homes. It was to be a peaceful demonstration of the power of the black community. It would tell
the whole country that blacks felt strongly about the
indignities of racism.

The rally and the blackout were a success. Madison
Square Garden was full, and when Randolph entered the
huge hall behind an honor guard of Pullman porters and
maids he got a standing ovation that lasted for many
minutes. Speeches and entertainment took up most of the
evening, and the crowd thundered, "We are Americans
too." And Harlem that night was pitch-black, the only
lights showing were the streetlamps and automobile
headlights making their way down the silent streets.

Through these tactics, Randolph succeeded in building a mass movement that appealed to lower class working people as much as it did to the professional and
middle class blacks who were members of the NAACP.
Randolph traveled far and wide during the war, helping
to organize March committees in many cities. The coun-

try was at war, and while he still threatened a mass march on Washington, wartime travel restrictions and the mood of the country made it impossible for such an event to occur. But he hoped to have an effect upon the government's policies by raising the threat of a March and by demonstrations in the big cities.

One of the first concerns of the movement was to make sure that the FEPC enforced the President's ban on discrimination. In fact, the fight to make that agency strong started immediately. It was decided that the members of the FEPC would be drawn from labor, business, and the public. When the administration proposed naming two little-known labor leaders to serve on it, Randolph fired off a telegram to the White House threatening to revive his plans for a march on the capital if the labor representatives were not the presidents of the AFL and the CIO. Only men of such power and stature, he said, could ensure that the FEPC would be truly independent. Roosevelt recognized Randolph's importance by agreeing to his demand and by offering him a place on the committee. But Randolph refused, saying he preferred to remain outside it, where he could still speak out publicly. So his friend, Brotherhood vice-president Milton Webster, was appointed in his place.

Most government and business officials regarded the FEPC as a nuisance, and the committee spent much of the war in a fight for its existence. Political pressures often led it to cancel hearings to investigate charges of discrimination. It was often caught up in Washington power struggles and instead of being the all-powerful instrument Randolph had hoped for, it was under constant threat of being made part of other government agencies less sympathetic to fighting discrimination. But the

FEPC was able to be effective, and whenever its independence was threatened, Randolph would make strong public statements and call "SAVE FEPC" rallies.

At the war's end Randolph formed the National Committee for a Permanent FEPC to fight for its continuation. But Congress, in the grip of conservative Southerners, was against it, and the March movement's pressures were never as strong as the political pressures from the South.

Sometimes the March movement turned to defense of individual blacks trapped in the South's racism. It was a key part of the drive to save Odell Waller. Waller was a black sharecropper who was accused of killing his landlord in a dispute over payment for crop shares. But this was not a simple murder case. It symbolized the oppression of the sharecrop system that kept black farm workers chained to semi-slavery. The jury that convicted him was all white, since juries in Virginia were made up of voters, and the poll tax kept nearly all blacks from voting.

Randolph and other black leaders attacked the all-white jury system as unconstitutional, a view that would be upheld by the Supreme Court two decades later. But the courts refused their appeals and Waller was executed in July 1942. The New York branch of the March on Washington movement held a silent protest parade of five hundred blacks who marched to muffled drums, demonstrating their anger and their sorrow.

The Waller case was a dramatic example of the racism rampant on the home front during the war. Jim Crow still ruled over large parts of the country and racism was often cloaked in patriotism. A sign in a Charleston, South Carolina, bus read:

Victory demands your cooperation. If the peoples of this country's races do not pull together, Victory is lost. We, therefore, respectfully direct your attention to the laws and customs of the state in regard to segregation. Your cooperation in carrying them out will make the war shorter and Victory sooner. Avoid friction. Be Patriotic. White passengers will be seated from front to rear; colored passengers from rear to front.

In 1942 a Detroit mob prevented three black families from moving into a housing project. A year later, riots broke out all over the country. It was the "Red Summer" on a lesser scale. In Detroit, thirty-four people were killed in a murderous outbreak of violence that only ended when federal troops were called in. Harlem exploded too, and so did Los Angeles, Mobile, and Beaumont, Texas. In many instances, white resentment at black workers was the spark that caused the riots.

The crowning insult to most black Americans occurred when it became known that German prisoners of war, traveling to prison camps in the South, were allowed into railroad dining cars while their black guards and black civilian passengers were not. Blacks in uniform were rigidly segregated, both on and off army bases. Since most training camps were in the South, black soldiers had to endure the indignities of local segregation laws and, occasionally, the brutalities of racist attacks.

Most black servicemen were kept in segregated labor battalions, just as in World War I. Almost three out of four black soldiers were laborers, truck drivers, and supply men. Despite the attempt to shut them out of fighting units, black soldiers compiled a heroic record.

Black truck drivers kept the famous Burma Road open under constant Japanese attacks, and on the European front, black volunteers helped to win the Battle of the Bulge, fighting off Germany's last massive offensive.

Despite this, the armed forces insisted on segregation and continued to look down on black fighting men. Southern officers, many of them with racist attitudes, were appointed to command black troops. Blacks were shut out of high command positions. General Davis was the only black among the 776 generals, and there were only 7 black colonels out of 5,220. At the height of the war, Judge William Hastie, the War Department's civilian in charge of department policies affecting blacks, quit his job in disgust at this official racism.

Many black soldiers felt the same way, but they didn't have the right to quit. They stayed in uniform, did their jobs, and let their resentments and anger build. One black soldier wrote the NAACP from a Pacific island: "Just carve on my tombstone 'Here lies a black man killed fighting a yellow man for the protection of a white man.' "

It was to ensure that black men never again would have to write with their pens dipped in such sadness that A. Philip Randolph waged his next great fight for justice.

CHAPTER ELEVEN

End of the Jim Crow Army

THE war ended with the giant atomic mushroom clouds over Hiroshima and Nagasaki. Half a million black servicemen returned home to look for jobs, find housing, and go back to school. But Phil Randolph's war on their behalf was just entering a new phase.

The war's end brought the end of the March on Washington movement. Randolph believed that the organization had achieved its purpose of carrying on the fight against discrimination during the war. Now he felt the established civil rights agencies such as the NAACP and the Urban League should carry the ball. His concern was to battle for another of the war's casualties, the FEPC, which was also ended, since it was only ordered as an emergency wartime measure.

To carry on this fight, Randolph headed up a broad coalition of blacks, liberals, and labor leaders called the National Council for a Permanent FEPC. The success of the wartime FEPC led many people to support legislation to create a permanent body that would fight against job discrimination. Congress was still against it, but many states and cities passed their own Fair Employment Practices Committees. Randolph knew, however, that these would not be as effective as a national FEPC, and he kept fighting for one. When President Harry S Truman, who succeeded Roosevelt, seemed reluctant to support anti-discrimination efforts, Randolph even started a new People's party that planned to run candidates for office.

He had no personal political ambitions. In 1944 community leaders in Harlem asked him to be a candidate for Congress, but he refused. The new party he started in 1946 was meant to put greater pressure on the President and on the Democratic party to follow more liberal policies. When, in the following years, the President took up the cause of civil rights, Randolph gave up the idea of a new party.

But he did not give up the idea that the armed forces must be integrated. He fought against the Jim Crow army in two world wars, and lost his fight for army integration in 1941 only because it seemed more important to get the executive order against job discrimination. Then, in 1947, with the scars of prejudice and humiliation still fresh in the minds of black veterans, the time had come to launch an all-out fight on army segregation.

The fight against the Jim Crow army was triggered by the government's proposal to institute a peacetime draft. The hot war with Germany and Japan was over, but now there was a cold war with Russia, and the President wanted to build up the armed forces again. When the bill came before Congress it had no provision for integrating the army, which meant that young black men would once more be asked to wear their country's uniform while segregated into separate, inferior units. Randolph was determined that this should never happen again.

With Grant Reynolds, a New York State official, he organized the Committee Against Jim Crow in Military Service and Training, which was to be a pressure group to get the President and Congress to end segregation through the new draft law. This was Randolph's technique in action once more—he identified an issue, in this case the segregated army, and then formed a committee or coalition of interested groups to bring pressure on lawmakers. The March on Washington committee worked that way to win an FEPC, and now the new group would battle the army.

He had several meetings with Democratic leaders who promised that their party would do what it could. A powerful group within the government was also sympathetic to Randolph's demands. A presidential Committee on Civil Rights issued a report that called for an immediate end to discrimination in the armed services. Defense Secretary James Forrestal wanted to follow its recommendations, but he ran up against a stone wall in the form of the army chief of staff, General Omar Bradley, and other service chiefs who were against it.

That's where matters stood on March 22, 1948, when Randolph led a delegation of black leaders into the White House for a special conference with President Truman. The President was urged to end army discrimination; he was told that it was unfair to ask black men to serve their country and then treat them as second-class citizens. "In my recent travels around the country," Randolph said, "I found Negroes in no mood to shoulder guns for democracy abroad while they are denied democracy here at home."

Truman blew up and started talking about the ideals of loyalty and patriotism. But Randolph stood firm. "If there is no change in the racial policies of the armed forces," he said, "I will be forced to lead a campaign of civil disobedience against it." Truman pointed to his planned civil rights program, which went much further than any before and which risked losing the South in the election that year. But Randolph would not be moved, and the conference ended on a note of discord.

A week later, Randolph joined with twenty black organizations who called for an immediate end to segregation and the firing of any public official "who fails to act against these evils." But the country really became aware that Randolph meant business when he testified before the Senate committee that was holding hearings on the new draft bill. He shocked the Congressmen when he told them:

I personally pledge myself to openly counsel, aid, and abet youth, both white and colored, to quarantine any Jim Crow conscription system, whether it bears the label Universal Military Training or Selective Service. From coast to coast . . . I shall call upon all colored veterans to join this Civil Disobedience movement and to recruit their younger brothers in an organized refusal to register.

Sensing the alarm this caused, he went on to explain:

No white man here has felt the sting of discrimination and segregation, Jim Crowism. As a matter of fact, I believe any one of you men would raise hell if you felt the indignities and injustices that are suffered in America. Right here in Washington, the capital of the nation, a Negro cannot go to a restaurant and get a sandwich, cannot go to a theater. Do you mean to say that a democracy is worth fighting for by black men which will treat them that way?

Senator Wayne Morse could barely believe what he was hearing. He sympathized with the cause of black Americans, but, like Truman, he believed in a higher loyalty—patriotism. If our country is attacked, Morse asked, would you still "recommend a course of civil disobedience to our government?"

"Yes," Randolph answered. "Because . . . it is in the interest of the soul of our country and I unhesitatingly and very adamantly hold that that is the only way by which we are going to be able to make America wake up and realize that we do not have democracy here as long as one black man is denied all of the rights enjoyed by all the white men in this country."

Morse asked what he thought the outcome of such a civil disobedience campaign would be. Randolph faced the issue squarely. "I would anticipate nationwide terrorism against Negroes who refused to participate in the armed forces, but I believe that that is the price we have to pay for democracy that we want. In other words, if there are sacrifices and sufferings, terrorism, concentration camps, whatever they may be, if that is the only way by which Negroes can get their democratic rights, I unhesitatingly say that we have to face it."

Gently, Senator Morse tried to get the witness to admit that he was, for all the nobility of his beliefs, counseling treason.

But Randolph answered:

We would participate in no overt acts against our Government, no overt acts of any kind. In other words, ours would be one of non-resistance. Ours would be one of non-cooperation; ours would be one of non-participation in the military forces of the country.

I want you to know that we would be willing to absorb the violence, to absorb the terrorism, to face the music, and to take whatever comes and we, as a matter of fact, consider that we are more loyal to our country than the people who perpetrate segregation and discrimination upon Negroes because of color or race.

I want it thoroughly understood that we would certainly not be guilty of any kind of overt act against the country but we would not participate in any military operation as segregation and Jim Crow slaves in the army.

Randolph promised, "we will relentlessly wage war on the Jim Crow armed forces program and against the Negroes and others participating in that program. That is our position," he said to a hearing room hushed by the force of his determination and the unprecedented challenge it meant to the government and to the laws of the land. "However the law may be construed," Randolph ended, "we would be willing to face it on the grounds that our actions would be in obedience and in conformity with the higher law of righteousness than that set forth in the so-called law of treason."

Many black leaders were upset by such a radical stand. Some, including his old friend Walter White, opposed Randolph, and even the black press published editorials against his campaign for civil disobedience. It was one thing to march and demonstrate; it was quite another to refuse to serve in the armed forces and to counsel what the law defined as treason.

As always, Randolph's main support came from the black men and women who lived in poverty and who had no business or professional interests to protect by playing it safe. A survey among blacks in New York City found a majority agreed with Randolph so long as the country wasn't in a "hot" war. Another poll of black college students found that seven out of ten favored civil disobedience against the draft.

Within weeks, Randolph built a strong, grass roots organization, the League for Non-Violent Civil Disobedience Against Military Segregation, whose aim was to get young men to pledge that they would not serve if drafted into a Jim Crow army. Ghetto neighborhoods were plastered with leaflets against the draft, street-corner tables were manned by people gathering signatures on petitions protesting segregation, sound trucks slowly crept down the streets of black neighborhoods, their loudspeakers blaring jazz to attract attention, and then brief speeches against Jim Crow to fire up the crowds that gathered.

Randolph himself spoke to rallies in dozens of cities. "We will fill up the jails with young men who refuse to serve," he declared. "And I am prepared to fight the Jim Crow army even if I am convicted of treason and have to rot in jail. The time has come when we can no longer fight under the flag of segregation. We will no longer give aid and comfort to our enemies." To the men in Washington, A. Philip Randolph was once more, "the most dangerous Negro in the United States."

Just as he was personally willing to accept the consequences of his actions, Randolph was careful to explain the dangers of draft resistance to young Negroes. "If you refuse to be drafted," he told them, "you must be prepared to go to jail. We are fighting to pressure the President into issuing an executive order banning discrimination in the armed forces. Think carefully about what you do, because when we get our executive order, we will have achieved our goals and will disband. You may have to remain in prison. It is a tremendous sacrifice, so think about it. But if you decide to do it, you will be helping all black people take a step closer to freedom."

He was creating a very serious problem for the Truman administration. Organized black defiance of the draft would result in a national crisis. Further, the presidential elections were only months away, and everyone was predicting a Republican victory. Truman needed the black votes that might swing a close election. He could not afford open hostility from black voters, and Randolph's campaign was increasing black dissatisfaction with the President.

Finally, on July 26, Truman acted. He issued Executive Order 9981, which declared "that there shall be equality of treatment and opportunity for all persons in the armed services without regard to race, color, religion, or national origin. This policy shall be put into effect as rapidly as possible. . . ." The order set up a President's Committee on Equality of Treatment and Opportunity in the Armed Services, charged to recommend action to implement the new policy.

But Randolph still wasn't happy. The order didn't specifically state that segregation would end, it merely spoke of "equality of treatment and opportunity," which could be interpreted in many ways. And there was no firm deadline for integration. He refused to cease his activities against the draft until the White House sent a high official to promise him that the new presidential committee would end discrimination. Satisfied that the order would be implemented to end Jim Crow, Randolph agreed to call off his campaign.

Victory was once more won through militant, nonviolent action. Twice in the space of seven years, Randolph had forced two Presidents to issue historic executive orders giving black people their rights.

But some of the young militants in Randolph's organization were unhappy. One of them was Bayard Rustin, who had joined forces with Randolph during the March on Washington campaign, and was his right-hand man in the draft resistance. When Randolph called Rustin and the other anti-draft workers into his office to announce that the executive order meant that their organization would now be dissolved, they protested. "We should continue our campaign until the young men who have been jailed are released," they said. "I'm sorry," Randolph answered. "Those men knew the risks they were taking. We made a solemn pledge that when an executive order is issued, we would disband."

He asked Rustin to call a press conference for the following day so that he could make a public announcement of the end of his campaign. Rustin did so, but also called a press conference of his own. There, he and other young militants denounced Randolph for selling out. The campaign ended on this bitter note. Randolph was deeply hurt, but he understood the young men's feelings. He recalled his own youth when, in the pages of *The Messenger,* he had attacked older civil rights leaders in much the same way.

Rustin regretted what he had done. He respected Mr. Randolph, loved him, and as the weeks passed he became very ashamed of his actions. It took two years, but he finally decided to apologize personally. He came to Randolph's office and knocked hesitantly at the door. As he stepped into the cluttered room, Randolph left his desk and walked across to greet Rustin. "Why, Bayard," he said with surprised pleasure, "where have you been? You know I needed you." The older man and the younger one embraced, and resumed their comradeship.

There were others who were unhappy with the executive order too, but they were people who feared the end of segregation. General Bradley, for example, angrily declared that the army was no place to conduct social experiments. When the committee appointed by Truman began its work, it found stiff resistance from the military commanders. But Truman was behind the new policy. At his first meeting with the committee, he told them: "I'm with you all the way. If I have to knock some heads together to get the action you need, I'll knock heads together."

By 1950 the armed forces were well on the way toward integration. The air force, navy, and marines all moved quickly to integrate their units. The army was slower to do so, but then the Korean War broke out, and in 1951 General Matthew Ridgeway ordered integration of all the forces under his command. Black troops proved that they could be superior combat forces in integrated units, and the army then moved to integrate other commands. By 1954 integration was complete in the armed forces.

Phil Randolph had helped to kill the evil institution of Jim Crow that had persisted throughout every war in the nation's history.

CHAPTER TWELVE

"Keep Up the Pressure"

WITH the guns of war booming across the shell-pocked hills of Korea, Randolph's thoughts turned once more to jobs for black people. World War II resulted in economic gains for black workers, thanks to the FEPC. Now he urged President Truman to create another FEPC as an emergency action to ensure that the wartime economy would not leave out its loyal black citizens.

Congress refused to pass the bill creating the FEPC and President Truman didn't want to follow Roosevelt's lead by issuing an executive order. The mood of the country was conservative, the Democratic party was split by a revolt of its Southerners, who thought the President had already done too much for civil rights, and Truman didn't want to take any steps that would make him more unpopular.

In February 1951 Truman ordered government departments to enforce non-discrimination clauses in their contracts, but this fell far short of what Randolph wanted. He joined forces with Walter White again and together they sent telegrams, letters, and petitions to the White House calling for an FEPC. On June 25, the tenth anniversary of the first FEPC order, seven governors declared Fair Employment Days, eight mayors publicly asked Truman to issue an executive order, and Randolph traveled to Hyde Park where he joined Walter White and Mrs. Roosevelt in a special ceremony at the graveside of the late President Roosevelt. But all this agitation had little effect on Truman. The wires and letters went unanswered.

In December, Truman issued another order. He created a new presidential Committee on Government Contract Compliance to recommend action to make sure that anti-discrimination policies were being carried out. This was as far as he would go. Although the special committee found that the policies were "almost forgotten, dead and buried under thousands of words of standard legal and technical language in government procurement contracts," it had no power to force changes. The new order and the committee it created were smoke screens to obscure Randolph's calls for an FEPC with teeth in it, and to give the public the illusion that the problem was being dealt with.

But Randolph was fighting the war against job discrimination on two fronts. His other battleground was the labor movement, and here he met with slow but sure success. Sections of the labor movement, especially the construction trade unions, still discriminate against black workers, but most of the rest of the labor movement has come around to Phil Randolph's way of thinking.

In 1955 the American Federation of Labor and the Congress of Industrial Organizations decided to end their long dispute and merge into one single labor federation, the AFL-CIO. Randolph saw this as an opportunity to win more gains for black workers. He joined forces with liberal unionists to fight for a strong declaration against labor discrimination in the new constitution for the merged labor federation.

He was successful. The AFL-CIO issued a statement that said that one of the main reasons for uniting was "to encourage all workers without regard to race, creed, color, national origin, or ancestry to share equally in the benefits of union organization." The new constitution set up a committee "to bring about at the earliest possible date the effective implementation of the principle . . . of non-discrimination." Further, the new labor group and its president, George Meany, took a strong public stand favoring civil rights legislation and action against Jim Crow in the South. Its civil rights department soon announced that it had convinced some all-white unions to accept black members, and the AFL-CIO convention urged all member unions to set up civil rights committees and to fight discrimination by employers.

In recognition of his role as "Mr. Black Labor," Randolph was chosen to be a vice president of the AFL-CIO, becoming the highest ranking black unionist in the country's history. For thirty years, Phil Randolph had been coming to labor conventions and making his appeals for justice for black workers. Now, at long last, his valiant efforts were beginning to pay off. But there was still a very long way to go, and he was impatient at the labor movement's slowness. While others saw all the progress that had been made, Randolph continued to hammer away at the problems that remained. He still insisted that unions that discriminated should be thrown out of the organized labor movement.

Some progress had been achieved, and some strong pro-civil-rights statements had been made. But Randolph wanted decisive action that would once and for all kill the poisonous weeds of Jim Crow that infected the labor movement. The showdown came in 1959 at the AFL-CIO convention in San Francisco. Vice President Randolph stepped to the speaker's platform with a spring in his walk and a brightness in his eyes that made the convention forget that this white-haired gentleman had just celebrated his seventieth birthday. At an age when other men were basking in retirement, Phil Randolph was carrying on his lifelong fight for the rights of black people.

As he spoke, his firm voice and resonant tones filled the large meeting hall. Yes, some progress has been made, he said, but it was not enough. He charged that the AFL-CIO had failed to support its civil rights committee. He pointed out that some unions had been expelled from the Federation because they were dominated by Communists or because their leaders were corrupt. Why then, should unions that are racist be allowed to remain in an organization that declared itself opposed to racial discrimination? he asked.

President Meany was a blunt Bronx plumber who wanted to work quietly to end discrimination among member unions. He didn't want a public battle that would make the labor movement look bad. He answered Randolph by saying that the AFL-CIO was making progress. "When I became secretary of the AFL in 1940," he said, "there were twenty unions that didn't accept Negroes, now there are only two. And there are now over a million and a half Negro union members."

This was the same line that others had used to answer

Randolph's charges in the past, but it would not work this time. It's not enough, Randolph answered. He called on Meany and the AFL-CIO to take immediate action against segregated local unions, against discrimination of blacks, and against unions that had many black members but kept blacks out of leadership positions. Then he leveled his guns on the Brotherhood of Railroad Firemen and the Brotherhood of Railroad Trainmen. If these two unions don't eliminate their white-only policies within six months, he said, they should be expelled from the AFL-CIO.

The delegates looked at one another and shrugged. "Here we go again," one man said. "I'm sick and tired of hearing that guy complain all the time." President George Meany was furious. His face red with anger, he spat out at Randolph: "Who the hell appointed you guardian of all the Negroes in America?"

Meany's outburst did what Randolph's speech alone might not have been able to do—it put the issue of union discrimination on the front pages of all the newspapers in the country. Blacks were especially outraged at the insult to Randolph, and letters and telegrams denouncing Meany poured into AFL-CIO headquarters. But this just made Meany and the rest of the AFL-CIO's leadership even angrier. Later, in 1961, the Federation's executive council publicly censured Randolph because, according to Meany, he was personally responsible for the "gap that has developed between organized labor and the Negro Community" and because Randolph had gotten "close to those militant groups."

Randolph was content to let the storm rage about him. Always a gentleman who refused to get into street brawls, he preferred not to trade insults. The NAACP's head,

Roy Wilkins, identified the real issue in the dispute when he declared:

"If such a gap exists it is because Mr. Meany and the AFL-CIO executive council have not taken the required action to eliminate the broad national pattern of anti-Negro practices that continues to exist in many significant sections of the American labor movement, even after . . . the merger and the endless promises to banish Jim Crow."

Randolph's response was his old technique of organizing for action. "Keep up the pressure," he would say. "Always keep up the pressure." Early in 1960 he organized a new group, the Negro American Labor Council. It was made up of black union members from all over the country, banding together to advance the cause of blacks within the labor movement. The NALC, Randolph said, was not a rival of the labor Federation, it was to be the voice of blacks within the AFL-CIO.

Labor's leadership wasn't happy about this new development. Once again Randolph was condemned for setting up an all-Negro organization. Once again he was charged with dividing the labor movement. But Randolph insisted that the NALC was no different from other ethnic labor groups. He told the founding convention:

"While the Negro American Labor Council rejects black nationalism as a doctrine and practice of racial separatism, it recognizes the fact that history has placed upon the Negro, and the Negro alone, the basic responsibility to complete the incompleted Civil War revolution through keeping the fires of freedom burning in the civil rights revolution."

Then, to calm the fears of those who saw the group as a

breakaway organization that would lead blacks out of the AFL-CIO, Randolph continued: "It is not a black Federation of Labor, it will not constitute a form of dual unionism, it is pro-AFL-CIO, it is pro-George Meany, it is pro-Walter Reuther. . . . It is concerned about the elimination of segregation in every area of the American labor movement."

He finished his address with a reference to George Meany's attack on him the year before that collapsed the meeting in laughter. "This organization was not founded," he said, "to prove that Phil Randolph speaks for the Negro of the United States."

The NALC became the cutting edge of Randolph's efforts to bring trade-union democracy to all. At first, labor's leadership was opposed to the new organization. Only Walter Reuther, head of the auto workers and the number-two man in the AFL-CIO, spoke to the founding convention. Others, including Meany, refused to attend. Later, however, Meany agreed to recognize the group as the legitimate spokesman for black unionists.

Through the Negro American Labor Council, Randolph was able to help organize black caucuses, or subgroups of black workers, within trade unions. The NALC managed to eliminate racial discrimination in a number of unions, and it set up training programs for black youth to qualify them for construction jobs. The NALC moved to integrate the musicians' union, which in many cities had separate black and white locals, and it furthered the organization of New York hospital workers. Randolph played an active part in the campaign to unionize the underpaid hospital workers, heading a committee that pressured Governor Nelson Rockefeller and the state legislature to pass a law, in 1963, permitting them to join unions. Throughout the sixties, Randolph's NALC manned picket lines, held meetings, and gradually helped to swing many labor unions into the movement for civil rights, while encouraging greater black participation in the union movement.

And Randolph's efforts at pressuring the high command of labor for changes were also beginning to yield results. Despite the harsh words he directed at Randolph, Meany was a fair man who honestly wanted to end union discrimination. Prodded by the NALC and the forceful Randolph, he issued directives ordering that unions hold meetings in integrated facilities, appointed a special commission to help member unions integrate, and got the last of the holdout unions to abolish its white-only clause. By the time the 1963 convention rolled around, he was able to report that out of the AFL-CIO's 55,000 member locals, only 172, in nineteen national unions, were still segregated. There was still much to be done, but a revolution in labor's ranks had taken place since the days when Randolph waged a single-handed battle against an openly racist labor movement.

The 1963 convention also passed a strong resolution on civil rights which led Randolph to say that "it firmly commits organized labor to a front-line role in the civil rights revolution. . . . It was," he said, "the strongest statement ever to come before a convention of the AFL-CIO." With Meany, Reuther, and other top leaders fighting for a strong civil rights bill before the Congress, it looked like organized labor was finally doing what Randolph had urged it to do for decades.

That was as it should be, he felt. Labor had to be better than anyone else. "The labor movement," he declared, "cannot afford to measure its achievements in the field of racial justice by the standards of other institutions. . . . It is not enough to compare ourselves favorably with government or management."

At long last, a mood of tranquillity hung over a labor convention. George Meany recognized Phil Randolph's great role in helping to turn the labor movement around on race. "I recall when we didn't have such an active interest in this field," he told the convention. "I recall when Phil Randolph, Milton Webster, and two or three of us would sit down during a convention and see how far we could go. . . . I know that Phil Randolph came here year after year, and made his speech, made his plea. He didn't have too much help. . . ."

The labor movement was joining the new American revolution that was sweeping the country. Black people were on the march for jobs, civil rights, and freedom. Phil Randolph's was no longer a lone voice in the wilderness. His brand of non-violent militancy had flowered into a nationwide civil rights movement that defied southern bigots and racist laws. The Supreme Court's 1954 decision outlawing school segregation triggered a series of anti-Jim Crow actions by blacks all over the South. Bus boycotts, sit-ins at lunch counters, and Freedom Rides to desegregate buses and trains all riveted the nation's attention to the struggle.

And out of the South, there rose a new leader, a young minister named Martin Luther King, Jr., whose courage and calmness under pressure, and whose speeches and sermons moved the hearts and minds of his people, rallied all blacks to the cause of winning civil rights.

Phil Randolph, well into his seventies, still played a vital role in the movement. Not only was Dr. King an apostle of the Gandhian creed of non-violent direct action first used on behalf of black people by Randolph, but he was drawn into the rights movement itself by a friend and follower of the labor leader's.

King was a young preacher in Montgomery, Alabama, in 1955 when Mrs. Rosa Parks, a seamstress, boarded a bus and took her seat. Her feet ached after a day of standing at her job in a department store. Soon the bus filled up and when some white passengers entered, the driver ordered black passengers to give up their seats. That was the law; that was Jim Crow in action.

But Rosa Parks stayed in her seat. She would not move and when she was hauled off to jail for breaking the law, she touched off the revolution that continues to this day. Montgomery's black people were furious at what had happened. The long pent-up anger at the Jim Crow regulations burst in a flood of indignation. One of the most respected black leaders in the town was E. D. Nixon, a porter who had been with Randolph through the fight for union recognition. It was Nixon, along with other black leaders in town, who formulated the strategy of a mass bus boycott. Montgomery's blacks refused to ride the buses until the Jim Crow regulations were repealed. Black people walked, formed car pools, and rode mules, but they would not ride. Nixon helped the young minister, Dr. King, who quickly became famous throughout the nation as the heroic leader of the boycott. And after victory was won, Dr. King went up and down the South, leading black people in their struggle for justice.

This struggle captured the country's imagination. As Randolph had always said, mass direct action would focus attention on the injustices done to black people and would create the conditions for change. By the early sixties, most white Americans had, thanks to Randolph's efforts, served in the armed forces alongside blacks and worked alongside them in factories. It no longer seemed fair to the majority of Americans for blacks to be denied the right to vote in the South, to be refused service in restaurants and lunch counters, or to be forced to go to separate schools.

King often came to see Randolph to get his advice about new campaigns he was planning. Randolph sent his disciple and comrade, Bayard Rustin, to help King set up his marches and demonstrations. The elderly labor leader was the moving force behind the new revolution of the young; he was the father of the civil rights movement.

In 1957 he even had the joy of seeing—at last—a march on Washington. King had organized a prayer pilgrimage to the nation's capital that attracted about twenty thousand people who assembled at the Lincoln Memorial to ask for increased federal action on the civil rights front.

But while the mushrooming civil rights movement was winning support and headlines, Randolph was becoming concerned that real progress for black people was simply not taking place. Most people were misled by successful attacks on Jim Crow in the South, but the facts of life for the masses of black people remained grim. In 1962 he addressed the convention of his Negro American Labor Council, and ran down the long list of indications that something even more drastic would have to be done. Nearly a decade after the Supreme Court ruled school segregation unconstitutional, he said, there were more black children in segregated schools than ever before. More blacks were unemployed and the average black family was making less money—in relation to white families—than a decade ago. No, Randolph said, in spite of the marches and small victories against segregation, there must be immediate action to win more and better jobs and wages for blacks.

Something drastic had to be done. But what? Blacks were protesting in the streets, in the courtrooms, and in the legislative halls of the nation. And still, conditions were worsening.

Then one day, A. Philip Randolph had another one of those ideas of his that helped change the course of history.

CHAPTER THIRTEEN

Marching for Jobs and Freedom

BAYARD RUSTIN remembers that it all started on a cold January morning in 1963. He and Randolph were having one of their regular conversations about the current scene, black history, and the long struggle for civil rights. Randolph was a walking encyclopedia of historical information, and throughout his long career he loved most those moments when he could sit with younger men and chat about philosophy and history. A generation of young black leaders had grown up to maturity absorbing his wisdom and charm. Rustin was one of those young men who had first come to talk and listen, and had stayed on to spend thirty years at the veteran campaigner's side.

Now, as the feeble rays of the winter sun slanted across the book-lined, paper-filled office, Randolph said: "You know, Bayard, we are coming to the end of an era."

"What do you mean by that, Mr. Randolph?" Rustin asked. Because of his age and his dignified bearing, even his closest associates called him "Mr. Randolph," although among themselves he was known affectionately as "the Chief."

Well, [Randolph replied] the revolution for dignity has been achieved. It may not seem so, because the brutalities of the Klan and the bigots are so painfully obvious still. But if we take a broader, historical view, Bayard, we can see that within the next year or so there will be a federal civil rights bill ordering complete desegregation. There will be a voting rights bill that will stop the South from keeping black people away from the polls. Dr. King and the young students, with their sit-ins and non-violent demonstrations, have created the national atmosphere whereby our civil rights and our dignity will shortly be achieved.

People will then have the right to go to restaurants and hotels that now keep blacks out. But they won't have the money in their pockets to make use of their newly won rights. The next stage of the struggle will be for economic advancement. I think if I were planning a march today, like the one I wanted back in 1941, it would be for jobs first, and freedom second.

The words hung in the cool air. Rustin let them sink in and then said: "I think that's a great idea. Why don't you have a march for jobs and freedom? I think it's important for people to know that we are at the end of one era and the beginning of another."

Randolph thought about it for a moment. The old warrior, now in his seventy-fourth year, felt the call to action once more. "Yes, Bayard," he said, "I think that's just what we'll do—one great, mighty demonstration that will close the period of demonstrations and inaugurate the era of economic confrontation.

"Why don't you get together with some of the young

fellows on our staff and draw up a plan for such a march? Yes, I believe that is what we will do."

A month later, the heads of all the major civil rights organizations found a letter from Phil Randolph on their desks. He was planning a mass March on Washington for Jobs and Freedom, the letter said, and he wanted them to join with him in bringing 100,000 blacks and whites to the capital. Some, like Dr. King, were enthusiastic. Others were cool to the idea. Some feared that such a giant march would just create enemies for black people. What if there were outbreaks of violence? Who knows what might happen with 100,000 people gathered together on a hot summer's day? The risks were great.

There was also a civil rights bill before the Congress. President John F. Kennedy had asked for sweeping civil rights reforms, but southern Congressmen, who dominated the committees that controlled legislation, were busy tying it up. The President's bill, many felt, was weak. But it should be passed and a mass demonstration might make important Congressmen angry. They might refuse to vote for such a bill if they felt that they were being pressured into it by 100,000 people in the streets.

But Randolph indicated he would mount a march anyway. The stragglers joined up. Randolph did not want personal glory; he wanted the March to include all people and organizations who had a stake in the fight for equal rights. By late spring he had assembled a broad coalition that included all of the black civil rights organizations, the major religious faiths, and the labor movement.

They all agreed that Randolph should be the director of the March, and he appointed Bayard Rustin, who had a genius for organization, as deputy director. It was

Rustin's job to make the detailed plans for assembling the huge crowd and to make sure that everything was in place for a successful demonstration.

It was an awesome job. As Rustin explained a few years later,

You start to organize a mass march by making an ugly assumption. You assume that everyone who is coming has the mentality of a three-year-old. You have to tell them every little detail of what they should do. So you can't just tell them to bring lunch along, you have to tell them what to put in it and what not to put in it. I went to a doctor friend of mine and I asked him, "What should people bring in a box lunch on a hot day in August?" And he told me, and then we instructed people to bring chicken or red meat, covered fruits like oranges or bananas, and to stay away from foods that would spoil, like fatty meats and mayonnaise. You don't want 100,000 people collapsing from food poisoning, do you?

Then you look at the facilities available to you. What can the Urban League do in organizing people in its cities? The NAACP? The labor and church groups? Each of the organizations joining with us had the ability to inform their members and friends about the March. They could gather people throughout the country and mobilize them to come to Washington.

And there had to be leaflets and booklets for every person who might want to come. They had to have detailed instructions on what to bring, where to assemble in Washington, what to do when they got there—even how to leave when the March ended.

Rustin and his staff, including representatives from the sponsoring organizations, worked out all the details. Every few days, he would bring the plans in to Randolph, who would look them over and offer suggestions, sometimes coming up with things that no one noticed.

"What about marshals for the March?" he would say. "Have you thought of asking black policemen from the big eastern cities to serve as marshals to keep order? You know, they could be a big help, and if they bring their families and friends, that would be even more people for the March."

A gentle man, Randolph did not fling out orders. He suggested ideas and mentioned possibilities. He let his staff work with a great deal of freedom. The next time they would meet, Randolph would say something like: "Well, have you had any success in getting those policemen?" He would never say, "Did you do what I told you to do?" Even under the swelling pressures of this great March, he remained considerate and gentle to all who worked with him.

By the start of the summer, the March was building to huge proportions. There was never any doubt that 100,000 or more people would come. All over the country, bus, train, and airplane companies were swamped with requests for chartered vehicles and for reservations for August 28, the day of the March. In the White House, President Kennedy was no happier about the idea of a mass demonstration than President Roosevelt had been twenty-two years earlier.

Early in June he met with Randolph and the other civil rights leaders. Once again, Phil Randolph walked through the iron gates leading to the White House. He had talked personally with every President since Calvin Coolidge. To all, he had pleaded for justice for black people. Sometimes he met with failure, sometimes with success. But every President for the past forty years knew that sooner or later, Phil Randolph would be on his doorstep asking him to take political risks on behalf of black citizens.

Unlike Roosevelt, Kennedy did not try to talk the leaders into calling off the March. It was too late for that. But he did want them to know that he was disturbed by it. "I am opposed to this March," he told them. "The risks are too great. There might be some violence, and that would set back the civil rights cause.

"We want success in Congress," he said, "not just a big show at the Capitol. Some of these people are just looking for an excuse to be against us. I don't want to give them an excuse to say, 'Yes, I'm for the civil rights bill, but I'm damned if I will vote for it at the point of a gun.'

"The Negroes are already in the streets," Randolph answered. "It is very likely impossible to get them off. If they are bound to be in the streets in any case, is it not better that they be led by organizations dedicated to civil rights and disciplined by struggle rather than to leave them to other leaders who care neither about civil rights nor non-violence?"

Then Dr. King spoke up. The March, he said, "could also serve as a means of dramatizing the issue and mobilizing support in parts of the country which don't know the problem at first hand. I think it will serve a purpose. It may seem ill-timed. Frankly, I have never engaged in any direct action which did not seem ill-timed."

Publicly, the President said he thought it was quite all right for citizens to come to Washington to petition the nation's leaders for action. It was their democratic right to do so, he declared. But privately, he still had misgivings about it. One wrong move, one violent act, and his whole civil rights program would fail and the country would become fed up with black protests. Who knew what would happen then?

The great day arrived. On the morning of August 28 it seemed as if every road leading into Washington, and every train and air terminal, was packed with people coming for the March. Washington had never seen anything like it. An endless stream of people flowed into the city bearing signs, buttons, and banners proclaiming their demand for jobs and freedom.

Randolph spent the early morning meeting with important Congressmen, many of whom would join the March. Behind the White House, on the grassy lawns beside the broad reflecting pool that stretches from the Lincoln Memorial to the Washington Monument, crowds of people were gathering. By noon, the entire area was a sea of faces. Like a checkerboard, blacks and whites were intermingled for as far as the eye could see. They sat and stood peacefully. The air was filled with songs; Joan Baez, Bob Dylan, Odetta, and other entertainers were there, singing of freedom and of the black martyrs to the cause of equality.

Phil Randolph looked out upon the multitude from the speakers' platform in front of the brooding statue of the Great Emancipator at the Lincoln Memorial. He had once dared to say that he could get 10,000 black people to come to this very spot to march for an FEPC. Now how many were there? Not 10,000, not 50,000, not 100,000, not even 150,000. There were 250,000 people massed in front of him, and at least 75,000 were white. Black and white were united for freedom, for the black man's rights, for the liberation of their common nation from the bonds of racism.

Randolph introduced each of the speakers in his clear, ringing voice. His powerful tones filled the huge clearing. Churchmen prayed and spoke of the moral struggle for civil rights. Black leaders talked of their fight for justice, Walter Reuther (George Meany, who was feuding with Reuther, didn't come) brought labor's backing. But the high point of the historic afternoon came when Martin Luther King, Jr., stepped to the podium and told of his dream. In the rich, rolling tones of the Baptist preacher, he intoned:

I have a dream that one day this nation will rise up and live out the true meaning of its creed: "We hold these truths to be self-evident; that all men are created equal!"

I have a dream that one day on the red hills of Georgia the sons of former slaves and the sons of former slave-owners will be able to sit down together at the table of brotherhood.

I have a dream that one day even the state of Mississippi, a desert state sweltering with the heat of injustice and oppression, will be transformed into an oasis of freedom and justice.

I have a dream that my four little children will one day live in a nation where they will not be judged by the color of their skin but by the content of their character.

I have a dream today.

With each "I have a dream" the huge crowd thundered its approval—250,000 voices were raised in great cheers.

This is our hope [Dr. King continued]. This is the faith with which I return to the South. With this faith, we will be able to hew out of the mountain of despair a stone of hope. With this faith, we will be able to transform the jangling discords of our nation into a beautiful symphony of brother-hood. With this faith, we will be able to work together, to pray together, to struggle together, to go to jail together, to stand up for freedom together, knowing that we will be free one day.

Let freedom ring.

When we let freedom ring, when we let it ring from every village and every hamlet, from every state and every city, we will be able to speed up that day when all of God's children, black men and white men, Jews and Gentiles, Protestants and Catholics, will be able to join hands and sing in the words of the old Negro spiritual, "Free at last! free at last! thank God almighty, we are free at last!"

King's dramatic speech stirred the nation's soul. Millions were watching it on television, and his great, idealistic dream has become a part of the nation's heritage, as familiar as the Gettysburg Address or Washington's Farewell Address. Thousands were moved to tears, thousands were numb with the vision of his dream. The masses crowded before the Memorial released their pent-up emotions with a tumultuous ovation.

When Randolph strode before them once more, they all knew they were making history. Bayard Rustin read the Demands of the March, a ten-point program calling for jobs and an end to discrimination in all its forms. And then Randolph recited the Pledge, in which the massive assemblage pledged a personal commitment to continue to fight for social justice "until victory is won." "I do so pledge," the huge crowd thundered, and their pledge was not to be dismissed by the White House, where the President watched the proceedings on television, the sounds of the television set mixing with the "live" roar of the crowd several hundred yards from his window. At a meeting with the March's leaders later in the day, he expressed his relief that all went well, and promised to fight for the civil rights bill.

Nor was it lost on the Congress either, many of whose members were present at the Lincoln Memorial. Some Congressmen went back to work on the bill, decided it was too weak, and in 1964 passed the strongest civil rights bill in history. It barred discrimination in most public places such as restaurants and hotels, increased the government's power to fight discrimination in the schools and other public facilities, and it required an end to discrimination in federally assisted programs, including employment discrimination. The following year, it passed a Voting Rights Act that ensured black Southerners the right to vote.

Throughout the difficult political negotiations leading to these victories, the President and the Congressmen constantly had before them the vivid memories of that glorious day in August. The March proved that blacks and whites could join together for common goals, and that non-violent action could produce results. In the years to come, the interracial coalition grew strained and outbreaks of violence took place. But August 1963 marked the high point of the civil rights movement, and Randolph's March put the government squarely behind a program of broad social change.

As the long day drew to a close, Phil Randolph stood watching the enormous crowd move slowly away, to the buses, cars, trains, and planes that would take them back home. The day was ending, the day he had dreamed of for so many years. Bayard Rustin walked over to where he stood, off to the side of the Memorial. Together they watched the last of the great throng recede into the distance.

"Mr. Randolph," Rustin said quietly, "it looks like your dream has come true."

Randolph did not answer, but as he stood there in silence, tears were streaming down his cheeks.

CHAPTER FOURTEEN

Father of the Civil Rights Movement

THE decade that followed the great March on Washington found A. Philip Randolph still active, setting a pace that would tax a much younger man.

He was still building coalitions with other groups to advance the cause of black people. In 1968, he became co-chairman of the Urban Coalition, a broadly based group of some of the most important business and civic leaders in the country who banded together to help find a solution to the nation's urban problems. He also served as a leader of the American Committee on Africa, an organization dedicated to building better relations with the independent black states just emerging from colonial rule. Randolph also has been outspoken in condemning the racism of South Africa and other territories where blacks are denied their civil rights and their independence.

He remained active in the labor movement as well. Although ill health led him to retire as president of the Brotherhood of Sleeping Car Porters, he stayed on as an

AFL-CIO vice president and kept insisting that the labor movement include underprivileged workers. He helped build trade-union support for the new union of West Coast migrant farm laborers and for black hospital workers in the South. In 1971, at the age of eighty-two, he helped to launch a new drive to unionize household workers.

Much of his civil rights activity centered about the A. Philip Randolph Institute, founded in 1964 to fight for black equality and for fulfillment of his lifelong dream of building solid black participation in the labor movement. With Randolph as president and Bayard Rustin as executive director, the Institute built a network of affiliates spanning the nation. It conducts a wide variety of programs, but is best known for its successful efforts to recruit and train black youths for construction-trade jobs, and for its role in breaking down discriminatory trade-union barriers.

In the fullness of his age, honors continued to shower upon him. In 1964 President Lyndon B. Johnson awarded him the Medal of Freedom, the nation's highest civilian honor. As Phil Randolph received his medal in an impressive White House ceremony, he thought of how often he had been to this presidential mansion—to pressure, cajole, and convince seven American Presidents. Inscribed on the award was the tribute: "Through four decades of challenge and achievement, he has led his people and his nation in the great forward march to freedom."

In 1966 President Johnson appointed him honorary chairman of a special White House Conference on Civil Rights. "In the near future," Randolph told the meeting of rights workers, labor and business leaders, and govern-

ment officials, "I shall call upon the leaders of the Freedom Movement to meet together with economists and
social scientists in order to work out a specific and docu-
mented 'Freedom Budget.' I shall submit these recommendations to the President."

Phil Randolph was as good as his word. He had already
staged the "march to end all marches." Now he knew that
it was necessary to lay a blueprint before the nation, a
master plan to achieve equality. Under the sponsorship of
his Institute, he gathered together a broad group of
experts to come up with just such a blueprint, and then
he got a star-studded list of more than two hundred
prominent people and civil rights groups to endorse it.

The result, the "Freedom Budget for All Americans,"
was issued in 1966. It featured detailed suggestions for a
ten-year plan to end poverty, wipe out slums, ensure that
everyone who wants to work has a decent job, provide
health care for all, and keep the economy booming with
full production while cleaning up the environment. This
is a rich country, Randolph said, and it has the means "to
abolish poverty for the first time in human history." The
"Freedom Budget" was designed to show how the
country could achieve the goals of the 1963 March on
Washington.

Many people felt that the Freedom Budget, which
called for spending $185 billion over a ten-year period,
would be too costly. But Randolph pointed out that this
was really a modest sum compared with other expendi-
tures. The war in Vietnam cost twice as much over the
past ten years. "The question is not whether we have the
means," Randolph declared. "The question is whether
we have the will. Ten years from now, will two-fifths of
our nation still live in poverty and deprivation? This is,

above all, a moral question. And upon the answer hangs not only the fate of the Negro—weighed down by centuries of exploitation, degradation, and malice—but the fate of the nation."

Randolph's Freedom Budget has not yet been adopted. But the country took a long time to get around to accepting his other dreams too. It took a dozen years for his vision of a strong black porters' union to become a reality. It took forty years of constant pressure before he was able to end most union discrimination. It took nearly as long to bring about the fruition of his dream of an awakened black citizenry confident in its power and proud of its heritage. More than two decades passed before his dream of a giant March on Washington was fulfilled. Randolph has always been a generation or two ahead of his time and the Freedom Budget may also yet come to pass when the humane values he has championed are shared by the majority of American citizens.

Randolph has never accepted defeat. He stuck to his beliefs and his principles in the darkest hours of despair. He was a lone battler, mobilizing others to apply pressure to the vulnerable points of a society that had to change. He became famous, but he left the headlines to others, and never tried to use the causes he led to build personal power.

He started his public career as a radical critic of society, branded "the most dangerous Negro in America." In the twilight of his long career he was hailed as one of the great men of the nation. But *he* did not change; it was society that changed to absorb many of his convictions and demands. And a big reason for the change in society was A. Philip Randolph's constant, unceasing effort to win equality for black people. He gave up the oppor-

tunity to gain personal wealth and fame, accepting the
poverty and unpopularity of those who remain outside
critics of society's power centers, trying to change them.
He risked jail, beatings, and powerful enemies to remain
true to his cause.

The list of Randolph's accomplishments is truly awesome. He built a union of black workers when no one
thought it could be done. He helped to desegregate a
labor movement that had been one of racism's strongholds. He forced the creation of a wartime FEPC, defying
a President of the United States to do so. He defied
another President to end segregation in the armed forces.
He laid the strategy for the successful non-violent civil
rights movement of the sixties which helped to expand
the rights of all black people.

Every single black man who works for a living, who
joins a union, who serves in the armed forces, or who is
now free to use a former Jim Crow facility can stand
taller and straighter because A. Philip Randolph spent
his life fighting for black equality and won great victories. Throughout his long life he has led the cause of
black Americans, binding their concerns with the cause
of all the country's poor and unprivileged. It was Randolph who laid the broad strategies others have followed,
and it was Randolph who provided the philosophic and
economic framework for generations of civil rights
fighters. He was indeed the father of the civil rights
movement.

Always concerned with young people, he has nurtured
generations of future leaders with the wisdom of his
experience and knowledge. Never content with basking
in his victories, he has always moved on to the next stage

of problems confronting black people. He always remained concerned about the economic aspects of the fight
for freedom. To the youth of today he said, in 1969:

The youngsters of today must direct their attention not
only to the matter of racial identity and racial realization
through African studies, but they must make certain they are
not left behind in the scientific and technological revolution,
because if they are, they will be in a hopeless state. There will
be absolutely no way in the world whereby they can become
an effective force. If the young Negro cannot become a part
of this advancing technology, his whole revolution will have
been in vain.

Early in 1969 Mr. Randolph celebrated his eightieth
birthday. The venerable father of the civil rights movement had many friends who wanted to honor him on that
great occasion, and so the Waldorf-Astoria Hotel in New
York was the site of an Eightieth Birthday Dinner. Dig-
nitaries came from far and wide. One of the richest men
in the world, New York's Governor Nelson Rockefeller,
came to pay tribute to the militant Socialist editor of *The
Messenger*. AFL-CIO President George Meany came to
honor his colleague, who was often a friend and often a
foe. Mr. Randolph's brothers in the civil rights movement left their picket lines and their offices to be with
him that night. The glittering assemblage included politicians and businessmen, labor leaders and government
officials, old people and youngsters, and the black people
and working people to whose cause he had dedicated his
long life.

Speaker after speaker rose and told of the greatness of

A. Philip Randolph, as the quiet, modest man who had done so much to help so many sat, head bowed, listening to the honors his friends were heaping upon him. Then, Phil Randolph stood, and in the voice that was so familiar from the public battles of half a century, told the audience:

Our gathering here tonight is an honoring, and for that I am deeply grateful and humbled. But in a more profound sense it is a rededication—to a cause to which I have contributed my energies, and to principles to which I have dedicated my life.

The cause has been the liberation of the Negro in America. I have seen fit in this endeavor to try to establish an alliance between the Negro and the American trade-union movement. I have been guided by the belief that Negroes are a working people, and that because of their history on American soil—a history of suffering and tragedy, but also of struggle, endurance, dignity, and, ultimately, a history of human triumph —that because of this history they have been a dispossessed people who have often had to migrate thousands of miles in search of the means of subsistence. The labor movement has been the home of the workingman, and traditionally it has been the only haven for the dispossessed. And, therefore, I have tried to build an alliance between the Negro and the American labor movement.

I have not been alone in my efforts. In 1925, almost half a century ago, I and my colleagues founded the Brotherhood of Sleeping Car Porters. In our struggle to build the union we faced destitution and continual harassment, but we did build it, and our struggle conferred upon us collectively a certain dignity. With this victory, my brothers and I in the union not only improved the conditions under which we lived and worked, but we were enabled to reach beyond ourselves to our brothers and sisters on the plantations and in the ghettos. We were able to reach out and build a movement of the Negro masses struggling to realize, upon this American soil, the freedom and the justice which they had so long been denied.

In my life I have tried to abide by the principles of democracy, non-violence, and integration. We cannot reject these principles without also denying ourselves the possibility of freedom.

Salvation for the Negro masses must come from within. Freedom is never granted; it is won. Justice is never given; it is exacted. But in our struggle we must draw for strength upon something that far transcends the boundaries of race. We must draw upon the capacity of human beings to act with humanity towards one another. We must draw upon the human potential for kindness and decency. And we must have faith that this society, divided by race and by class, and subject to profound social pressures, can one day become a nation of equals, and banish white racism and black racism and anti-Semitism to the limbo of oblivion from which they shall never emerge.

Selected Bibliography

A Freedom Budget for All Americans, New York: A. Philip Randolph Institute, 1966.

Berman, William C. *The Politics of Civil Rights in the Truman Administration.* Columbus: Ohio State University Press, 1971.

Brazeal, B. R. *The Brotherhood of Sleeping Car Porters.* New York: Harper & Bros., 1946.

Broderick, Francis L., and August Meier, eds. *Negro Protest Thought in the Twentieth Century.* Indianapolis: Bobbs-Merrill, 1965.

Buder, Stanley. *Pullman: An Experiment in Industrial Order and Community Planning.* New York: Oxford University Press, 1967.

Cayton, Horace, and George Mitchell. *Black Workers and the New Unions.* Chapel Hill: University of North Carolina Press, 1939.

Cronon, Edmund David. *Black Moses: The Story of Marcus Garvey and the Universal Negro Improvement Association.* Madison: University of Wisconsin Press, 1955.

Dalfiume, Richard M. *Desegregation of the U.S. Armed Forces.* Columbia: University of Missouri Press, 1969.

Draper, Theodore. *The Rediscovery of Black Nationalism.* New York: Viking Press, 1970.

Embree, Edwin R. *Thirteen Against the Odds.* New York: Viking Press, 1944.

Franklin, Charles L. *The Negro Unionist in New York.* New York: Columbia University Press, 1936.

Garfinkel, Herbert. *When Negroes March.* New York: Atheneum, 1969.

Greene, Lorenzo, and Carter Woodson. *The Negro Wage Earner.* New York: AMS Press, 1970.

Harris, Abram L., and Sterling D. Spero. *The Black Worker.* New York: Atheneum, 1968.

Jacobson, Julius, ed. *The Negro and the American Labor Movement.* Garden City, N.Y.: Anchor Books, 1968.

Kesselman, Louis C. *The Social Politics of FEPC.* Chapel Hill: University of North Carolina Press, 1948.

Lewis, Anthony. *Portrait of a Decade.* New York: Bantam Books, 1965.

Lewis, David L. *King: A Critical Biography.* New York: Praeger, 1970.

Lindsey, Almont. *The Pullman Strike.* Chicago: University of Chicago Press, 1963.

Logan, Rayford, ed. *What the Negro Wants.* Chapel Hill: University of North Carolina Press, 1944.

Marshall, Roy. *The Negro Worker.* New York: Random House, 1967.

Murray, Robert K. *Red Scare.* New York: McGraw-Hill, 1964.

Northrup, Herbert R. *Organized Labor and the Negro.* New York: Harper & Bros., 1944.

Osofsky, Gilbert. *Harlem: The Making of a Ghetto.* New York, Harper & Row, 1966.

Ottley, Roi, and William Weatherby. *The Negro in New York: An Informal Social History 1626–1940.* New York: Praeger, 1969.

Parris, Guichard, and Lester Brooks. *Blacks in the City.* Boston: Little, Brown, 1971.

Record, Wilson. *The Negro and the Communist Party.* Chapel Hill: University of North Carolina Press, 1951.

Ross, Arthur M., and Herbert Hill, eds. *Employment, Race and Poverty.* New York: Harcourt, Brace & World, 1967.

Ruchames, Louis. *Race, Jobs and Politics.* New York: Columbia University Press, 1953.

Schuyler, George S. *Black and Conservative: The Autobiography of George S. Schuyler.* New Rochelle, N.Y.: Arlington House, 1966.

Sternsher, Bernard, ed. *The Negro in Depression and War.* Chicago: Quadrangle Books, 1969.

Stillman, Richard J. III. *Integration of the Negro in the U.S. Army.* New York: Praeger, 1968.

Taft, Philip. *Organized Labor in American History.* New York: Harper & Row, 1964.

Vincent, Theodore. *Black Power and the Garvey Movement.* San Francisco: Ramparts Press, 1971.

Waskow, Arthur I. *From Race Riot to Sit-In: 1919 and the 1960s.* Garden City, N.Y.: Anchor Books, 1967.

Weinstein, James. *Decline of Socialism 1912–1925.* New York: Vintage Books, 1969.

White, Walter. *A Man Called White.* New York: Viking Press, 1948.

Woodward, C. Vann. *The Strange Career of Jim Crow.* New York: Oxford University Press, 1966.

Index

AFL, 19, 87, 134–135. *See also* AFL-CIO

and Brotherhood of Sleeping Car Porters, 71, 72, 73

committee to investigate discrimination, 84

"federal" unions for blacks, 37, 72–73, 84, 86, 89

Harrison report, 85–86

racial policies, 35, 36, 37, 38, 73, 86

racial policies condemned, 33–34, 82

Randolph's efforts to end discrimination in, 83–84, 88–91

AFL-CIO, 134–140. *See also* AFL; CIO

African Methodist Episcopal Church, 4

American Committee on Africa, 156

American Federation of Labor. *See* AFL

A. Philip Randolph Institute, 157

auto workers' union, 87

Black Worker, The, 74

Boeing Aircraft, 101

Bowe, William, 45, 76

Bradley, Omar, 125, 132

Brotherhood of Locomotive Firemen and Engineers, 81

Brotherhood of Railroad Firemen, 137

Brotherhood of Railroad Trainmen, 137

Brotherhood of Sleeping Car Porters, 50–51, 58–59, 68–69, 70–71, 74

admission to AFL, 72–73

and argument against tipping, 61–62

Brotherhood of Sleeping Car Porters *(continued)*
attempts of white unions to absorb, 71, 73
attitude of black community toward, 56–57
becomes legal representative of porters, 75–76
establishment of, 45–48
first demands to Pullman Company, 48–49
and Mediation Board, 60, 64–65
negotiations with Pullman Company, 77–78
Pullman Company's efforts against, 52–55
and Railway Labor Act, 75
and strike against Pullman Company, 63–64, 66–68
Broun, Heywood, 61
Bunche, Ralph, 93

Chicago *Defender,* 57
Chicago *Whip,* 57
CIO, 87, 95, 134–135. *See also* AFL-CIO
Cohen, Morris Raphael, 12
Committee Against Jim Crow in Military Service and Training, 125
Committee on Civil Rights, 125
Committee on Government Contract Compliance, 134
Communists
attitude of Randolph toward, 23, 31, 33, 55, 95, 116

and National Negro Congress, 95, 96–98
party line, 96, 97, 116
and unions, 136
Congress of Industrial Organizations. *See* CIO
Coolidge, Calvin, 31–32, 62–63
Crosswaith, Frank, 47, 103

Daily Worker, 116
Davis, Benjamin O., 102, 122
Davis, John P., 93, 94
Dellums, C. L., 47, 77
Democratic party, 12–13, 124, 133
Des Verney, W. H., 45, 46, 47
Du Bois, W. E. B., 9–10, 18, 19, 37

electricians' union, 51
Employee Representation Plan. *See* Pullman Company, company union

Fair Employment Practices Committee (FEPC), 109, 119–120, 123–124, 133–134
Farmer, James, *112ff.*
Ford, James W., 96
Forrestal, James, 125
"Freedom Budget," 158–159
Friends of Negro Freedom, 28

Gandhi, Mahatma, 117
Garvey, Marcus, 28–29, 30. *See also* Marcus Garvey movement
Gompers, Samuel, 35–36, 37–38

Great Depression, 74, 80–81, 99
Green, William, 66–68, 71, 73, 75, 81, 85, 86, 90

Harding, Warren, 28
Harlem Renaissance, 27
Harrison, George, 85, 86
Hastie, William, 122
Headwaiters and Sidewaiters Society of Greater New York, 15
Hill, T. Arnold, 101
Hilquit, Morris, 30
Hitler, Adolf, 96–97
hotel alliance, 71–72
Hotel Messenger, The, 15–16
Hughes, Langston, 80

Industrial Workers of the World (IWW), 19, 33
Interstate Commerce Commission (ICC), 61

Johnson, James Weldon, 34
Johnson, Lyndon B., *112ff.,* 157

Kennedy, John F., *112ff.,* 147, 149, 150–151, 153, 154
King, Martin Luther, Jr., *112ff.,* 117, 141–142, 143, 146, 147, 150, 152–153
Ku Klux Klan, 5–6, 16, 29, 146

La Guardia, Fiorello, 92, 105–106, 109
League for Non-Violent Civil Disobedience Against Military Segregation, 129

Lewis, John L., 87–88
Lincoln, Abraham, 30, 53
Lincoln, Robert T., 53
longshoremen's union, 39

March on Washington for Jobs and Equal Participation in National Defense (1941), 103–111
march movement, 114–120, 123
March on Washington for Jobs and Freedom (1963), *112ff.,* 146–155
Marcus Garvey movement, 28, 30, 31, 33. *See also* Garvey, Marcus
Meany, George, *112ff.,* 135, 136, 137, 139, 140, 141, 152, 161
Mediation Board, 60, 64, 75
Messenger, The
   barred from mails, 22–23
   and Brotherhood of Sleeping Car Porters, 45, 48, 57
   death of, 69
   financial troubles, 27–28
   as forum for attacks on Du Bois, 19
   as forum for attacks on Marcus Garvey, 29–30, 32–33
   as forum for attacks on World War I, 19–20
   as forum for Randolph's and Owen's answer to charges of Bolshevism, 24
   general editorial positions, 18, 22, 32–33, 38
   launched, 16–17

Messenger, The (continued)
and National Brotherhood
Workers of America, 39
offices raided, 24–25
slogans of, 16, 30–31, 32, 48
and Socialism, 30
Miller, Kelly, 95
mine workers' union, 37, 87
Moore, "Dad," 50
Morse, Wayne, 127
Murray, Philip, 95
musicians' union, 139

National Association for the
Advancement of Colored
People (NAACP), 18, 32,
95, 102, 123
National Association for the
Promotion of Labor Un-
ionism Among Negroes,
38–39
National Association of Ma-
chinists, 35, 36
National Brotherhood Work-
ers of America, 39
National Council for a Perma-
nent FEPC, 123
National Negro Congress
(NNC), 93–99
Negro American Labor Coun-
cil (NALC), 138–140
New Deal, 93–94
Nixon, E. D., 142

Order of Sleeping Car Conductors, 73
Owen, Chandler, 14, 29, 30
and *The Hotel Messenger*,
15

and *The Messenger*, 16, 19,
28, 31. *See also Messen-
ger, The*
and the Red Scare, 23, 24
and union organization efforts, 14, 28, 39

Palmer, A. Mitchell, 24
Parks, Rosa, 142
People's party, 124
President's Committee on
Equality of Treatment and
Opportunity in the Armed
Services, 130
Pullman Company, 41, 42, 45
and attacks on Randolph,
54, 69
and attempts to bribe Randolph, 70, 76
attitude toward unions, 43
and black press, 57
and Brotherhood of Sleeping
Car Porters, 50, 52–54, 56,
59–60, 62, 65, 69, 75, 77–78
company union, 44, 50, 60,
76
and strike threat, 65, 66–67
Pullman Porters Benefit Association, 44

race riots, 21–22, 32, 92–93, 121
Randolph, A. Philip, *112ff.*
attitude toward AFL, 19, 33–
34, 38, 71, 82
attitude toward Communists
and Communism, 23, 31,
33, 55, 95–98, 116

attitude toward World War I, 19–20, 21–22

attitude toward World War II, 113–114

and black pride, 58–59, 74

and Brotherhood of Sleeping Car Porters, 44–78

and capitalism, 12, 17, 21

and Du Bois, 9–10, 18

early life, 1–10

education, 6, 9, 11–12

and FEPC, 111, 119–120, 123–124, 133–134

and fight against discrimination in AFL and AFL-CIO, 71, 72–73, 83–87, 88–90, 135–141

and fight against discrimination in the armed forces, 101–102, 103–112, 114, 121–122, 124–132

and fight against job discrimination in government and industry, 101–109, 114–115, 118–120, 133–134

first years in New York City, 11, 13–14

and "Freedom Budget," 158–159

and Headwaiters and Sidewaiters Society of Greater New York, 15

honors, 111, 157

and *The Hotel Messenger,* 15–16

later life, 156–157

and March on Washington for Jobs and Equal Participation in National Defense (1941), 103–111, 114–120

and March on Washington for Jobs and Freedom (1963), 146–155

marriage, 26–27

and National Negro Congress, 93–99

and Negro American Labor Council, 138–140

and non-violent civil disobedience, 117, 126–129

opposition to Marcus Garvey movement, 28–30

and Pullman Company, 54, 69, 70, 76

as radical co-editor of *The Messenger,* 16–25, 27–34, 38–40

and Socialism, 12–13, 17–18, 28, 30, 32, 40, 57, 95

and trade unionism, 12, 13, 19, 40, 82

and union organization work, 13, 14, 28, 33, 38–39, 45 ff., 139

Randolph, James (brother), 1–4, 6–8

Randolph, James (father), 1–5, 6, 7, 9

Randolph, Mrs. James (mother), 1–2, 3, 4, 5, 6

Randolph, Lucille (wife), 26–27, 69

Rand School of Social Science, 30

Reconstruction, 5

Red Scare, 23–24

"Red Summer," 22, 28

Republican party, 12–13, 30

Reuther, Walter, *112ff.*, 139, 140, 152

Reynolds, Grant, *112ff.*, 125

Ridgeway, Matthew, 132

Rockefeller, Nelson, *112ff.*, 139, 161

Roosevelt, Eleanor, 105–106, *112ff.*, 134

Roosevelt, Franklin D., 74–75, 101–102, 106–109, 119

Rustin, Bayard, *112ff.*, 131–132, 143, 145–146, 147–149, 153, 154–155, 157

Socialists, 12–13, 28, 30, 95

Supreme Court, 6

Tampa Shipbuilding Corporation, 101

Totten, Ashley, 45, 46, 47, *112ff.*

Truman, Harry S, 124, 125–126, 130, 132, 133–134

Urban Coalition, 156

Urban League, 95, 123

Walker, A'Lelia, 27

Waller, Odell, 120

Washington, Booker T., 18

Webster, Milton P., 47, 119, 141

White, Walter, 102, 108, 128

   and attempts to create an FEPC, 133–134

   and March on Washington for Jobs and Equal Participation in National Defense, 103–111

   and National Negro Congress, 95

   and protest against segregation in the armed forces, 101

White House Conference on Civil Rights, 157

Wilkins, Roy, *112ff.*, 138

Wilson, Woodrow, 16

Young, Whitney M., Jr., *112ff.*